MW00980937

storyteller
UPRISING

Trust and Persuasion in the Digital Age

HANSON R. HOSEIN

Storyteller Uprising: Trust & Persuasion in the Digital Age

Copyright 2011 by Hanson R. Hosein.

All rights reserved.

Sixth Printed Edition, August 2012.

Published by HRH Media, Seattle WA.

ISBN-13: 978-1463631505

ISBN-10: 1463631502

i. Action Idea for this Project

With the decline of traditional journalism, there's an increased need for trusted information. This presents a huge opportunity to individuals, communities, companies and organizations. They can fill that void by telling their *own* multimedia stories and creating their *own* channels of distribution -- thereby serving as trusted sources in their *own* right. That's the "uprising" — people seizing control of communication by building ongoing credible connection through story and digital technology. *Storyteller Uprising* explains why this is now possible, and why you should harness the power of story in your own communication endeavors.

ii. Appreciation

Thanks to Sheetal Agarwal, Jay Al Hashal, William Mari Elizabeth Norville and Ashley Rose O'Mara for your assistance. Scott Macklin, Anita Verna Crofts, David Domke and Tim Fry were partners in the conspiracy to produce and promote this manifesto. My students and the University of Washington have been enthusiastically supportive. Gratitude to Roland, Shaffina and Ian Hosein as well as Melissa Nolas for unconditional support during that "long dark night." Dedicated to Heather Rae, Harper Rose and Hendrix Roland for your patience and inspiration – all my stories begin with you.

Cover concept by Theresa Stone, Monster Design. It contains a few of my images captured in Israel, Palestine, Iraq, Bahrain, the Persian Gulf, China, Seward NE, New Orleans, Detroit, New York City and Seattle. I'd like to recognize storytellers-in-arms Heather Hughes, John Liston, Kirk Mastin, Tom Powers and Scott Macklin for sharing some of these adventures with me.

Note: All hyperlinks in the printed edition of this book are easily accessible online at **http://www.storytelleruprising.com**.

TABLE OF CONTENTS

1. Telling Your Story -- Here's Mine

"Anyone can practice journalism," Dean Joan Konner said, on the first day of school at the Columbia University Graduate School of Journalism in September 1993. "And anyone usually does."

Most likely, Dean Konner intended that her words serve as a rallying cry for us, the chosen few who would bear the standard of professional journalism: well-trained, well-educated, armed with progressive ethics and principles. Newspaper readership was already in decline in the early 1990's, but that had little to do with a barely noticeable worldwide web. An explosion in cable news outlets and a number of other electronic sources of information made newspapers seem less timely, and necessary. Despite this competition and drop-off in audience, the writing would not appear on the wall for these print organizations for another fifteen years. At that point, they'd blame the Internet and profess to not have seen it coming.

Still, it was coming – even then. We just didn't know what to call this creeping sense of unease. Yes, there were more channels, more magazines – more content. But there was also more criticism, more declaration of mistrust of "The Media" as the citizenry would call this increasingly concentrated group of large corporations. Starting in the 1980's with deregulation, conglomerates would snap up the Big Three networks (ABC, CBC, NBC), competing newspapers folded into each other creating one-paper towns, and companies like Clear Channel would start programming radio stations from a central location thousands of miles away, dispensing with local DJ's in some cases. It's no coincidence that the public decline in trust in the American press began in 1985, according to a 2009 Pew Foundation study.

As I was set to graduate from Columbia, my colleagues and I looked out in dismay at what our professors were calling the "toughest" journalism job market that they could remember. So when NBC News unexpectedly offered me a job a couple of weeks prior to my graduation day, I figured it would be the best chance for me to land on my feet. One of my favorite professors had already called journalism the "first downwardly mobile profession," meaning I guessed, that I had better love what I did because the salaries just weren't going to get close to what a lawyer or an investment banker made.

I was fine with all of that – I was on a grand adventure. And though I had never watched much news on NBC, at least I'd have the benefit of working for a prestigious, and somewhat powerful, organization.

This sunny outlook was despite the fact that NBC was paying less than what I could afford to live on in pricey Manhattan, and without any health benefits whatsoever. An NBC News vice president would try to take the sting off of this hardship by proclaiming that more and more people would be flooding into journalism thanks to the proliferation of new distribution channels (primarily cable) like Headline News, CNBC, National Geographic, The Discovery Channel, which would only further depress salaries. He may have added that he was glad that he'd be retiring by the time the worst of this coming catastrophe would hit (he did).

Similar to Dean Konner's "everyone" declaration, this was still pre-Internet-as-mass-media slayer chatter. Non-linear editing software was too expensive for anyone but professionals and deep-pocketed hobbyists. If you didn't have six figures for a professional video or film camera, you were dabbling with decidedly consumer grade resolution with VHS, Super8 or 16mm. In the '90's, we were still in a mass media state of mind, deep within the heart of the world's media capital.

I would still get my chance to experience the power and glory of working in a top mass communications company, first as a producer at the still-flagship evening newscast, helmed by celebrated anchorman Tom Brokaw (ratings were already in decline from their 1980's nadir), and then on a prestigious overseas posting as the network's Middle East producer, based out of Tel Aviv, Israel. I was in my 20's – this was too good of an opportunity to pass up, and by the time they sent me to Israel, I was getting paid fairly well. Besides, I had the incredible opportunity to report firsthand on historical events.

Of course, it was an exciting life, working for a recognized American institution, within a country that appreciated American institutions. We would report on the news, sometimes produce features when the news cycle was slow, all overseen and vetted by management in New York. It was a simple process – someone would first pitch a story. From our end, it would either be a lead we had gleaned from a contact, or a nugget we had borrowed from the local news. From 30 Rockefeller Plaza, where NBC was headquartered, it'd more likely than not be something they had come across in the day's issue of the *New York Times*. We'd work up a story pitch, send it to New York, get approval to shoot the story (since it would cost us time, effort, and expense if we had to travel or hire freelance support), then head out as a foursome: producer, correspondent cameraman, soundman, maybe even a translator if we were going to interact with Palestinians. The team would shoot the story, return to our office to review the footage, write a script, get more approval from New York, then sit down with an editor to marry the images and sound to the script. Once we had finished the piece, we'd use an expensive satellite uplink to send the 2-minute story to "30 Rock" in time for the broadcast.

It was a tried and time-tested process, replete with several checks and balances, as well as with a number of creative contributors, all in support of a short piece of video that would air nationwide, and then end up in the archives.

I remember thinking that it seemed like an awful lot of effort for two pages of writing. And it felt all so transitory – even superficial – compared to the amount of work that we had put into produce so much content. Maybe ten percent of that content would end up in the final story.

And how could we gauge the impact of our work? Other than the requisite feedback that we'd receive from a colleague via the internal computer system, and the odd letter of complaint or support from a viewer or special interest group, many of our stories disappeared into the great news vacuum. Especially if it were breaking news, the average viewer would be hard-pressed to distinguish our work from the "alphabet soup" (CBS, ABC, CNN, and sometimes the BBC) of the other networks' output.

If the local people we had interviewed for the story wanted to see the final product, we would have to dub a copy to VHS tape. This was always an ordeal, as we would have to first convert the video from the American broadcast "NTSC" standard to "PAL" for the Middle East.

We always got access to the powerful players that mattered, within the military, government and militant groups. Sometimes, we would have to resort to the anchorman's star power to book a head-of-state or a charismatic, elusive leader like Yassir Arafat (who exuded "guerilla chic"). We knew what buttons to press, and were well aware of the rules of engagement if we wanted to sustain access to the subjects. When I once helped assemble a story that took a hard look at corruption and human rights abuses within the Arafat regime, we received an angry call from Brokaw just before his show went on the air, accusing us of maligning an American ally. Arafat was not Iraq's Saddam Hussein. It reminded me of that old adage, "he may be a son-of-a-bitch, but he's our son-of-a-bitch."

It was a cozy, insular, influential world. It was also very much a one-way communication environment, with little feedback.

My arrival in Israel coincided with the Dot Com boom, the 24-hour news craze, and the launch of news organization websites such as MSNBC.com. As I got the hang of my new job in the TV news world, I quickly discovered that I had a more substantive outlet in the less developed, less entrenched online one. Over the three and a half years that I would spend in the Middle East, I would increasingly spend my free time crafting web versions of the stories we were broadcasting, adding more detail, creating behind-the-scenes "Reporter's Notebooks," and eventually pitching more enterprising features for the .com team. Many of these stories were ones that I knew TV producers would never commit to, partly for financial reasons, mainly because they couldn't fathom how a mass audience would gravitate to what would translate to a small anecdote within a standard TV news story.

Other than the freedom to provide more detail, and thanks to developing digital imaging technology to provide my own images without having to rely on the efforts of a professional cameraman, I reveled in this ability to communicate directly with the audience (via an e-mail link at the end of my stories), and send behind-the-scenes missives to friends and family. I eventually purchased a broadcast-quality Sony digital video camcorder with my own funds, and used it to shoot still images (video file sizes were still too large, Internet access speeds, still too slow) that I would append to my "proto blog" – my very own online diary of life overseas as a network journalist. These were obviously still very early days, and I didn't tell too many of my colleagues about the "Hanson's Self-Center" site:

[http://aminstrel.tripod.com/]

I was probably still concerned about the appearance of "talking out of school" and potentially running counter to NBC's strict editorial policy. And perish the thought that I might not come across as "objective" – still the halcyon of mainstream American journalism.

It was already too late for me however. As I became further enamored with this more gratifying way of interpreting the news, which employed more subjective observation and reflection, as well as audience interaction, I grew increasingly frustrated with what felt like an editorial and creative straitjacket on the network side.

Near the end, NBC would award me stock options, as well as offer to promote me to serve its chief overseas producer based out of London. This happened after we produced a superb run of stories from the war in Kosovo in 1999. But this institutional recognition only filled me with a feeling of dread, and not one of elation. I knew I wasn't on the right track. I turned down the promotion, and then asked for the impossible. Would management allow a guy with the same last name (pronunciation-wise) as the dictator still in power in Iraq to take to the American airwaves as a correspondent, but primarily contributing to the network's flourishing web presence? I would experiment with more cost-effective, compact technology, and perhaps lead the way as the news organization contemplated the changing nature of the business ahead.

Their response was a quick and definitive, "no."

I was left with few options. Violence between Israelis and Palestinians was beginning to flare, as the second Intifada (Arabic for "uprising") was about to start. I had just convinced the woman who would soon become my wife to leave Seattle and move into my apartment in Tel Aviv. NBC presented me with two options: extend my stay in Israel another year, or return to the United States as a domestic news producer. There were no resources, interest or patience for an untested staffer like me to make the jump to become one of the public faces of America's top news network. My good fortune at the Peacock had run out. I was further weakened by a stress overload that put me in a Tel Aviv hospital with all the symptoms of a stroke. So when the network's foreign news editor asked me definitively whether I would renew my contract for another year, I was quick to decline. And then I resigned.

I was so determined to pursue another kind of creative path that I turned down attractive offers from Canadian TV networks to take national, on-air correspondent positions (ones that NBC would never had allowed me to fill). But to me, it felt like more of the same, with a defined institutional career path down the traditional road of journalism.

I ended up taking an unorthodox offer: an entry-level position at the Canadian Broadcasting Corporation, where I would learn how to shoot and edit my own stories from a one-person bureau in rural western Canada. It was the furthest thing from the top of the mountain, where I had been with NBC. It would be like being paid to go back to school. I could learn to master tools that didn't cost more than $10,000 cumulatively, and which I could stuff into a backpack, making me a portable broadcast studio. This approach suited the lesser-resourced public Canadian network well, despite the compromises it would have to make in production value with less professional gear, and this less trained professional.

I was awful at first. It was easy to distinguish between my grainy, dark footage and the sharp, smooth and steady video shot by a full-time cameraman. I had to aim the camera, ask questions, and reflect upon what other video elements I needed – strategizing throughout how I was going to edit it all together at the same time.

I loved the freedom to create, even as I chafed at being so far from the network's decision-makers in Toronto, leaving me out-of-sight, out-of-mind. The CBC was also less than enthusiastic about my request to create an online portal for my stories and behind-the-scene essays. So when George W. Bush began to threaten Iraq in 2002, and the network told me that it had no inclination to send anyone to the region other than their seasoned correspondents with their professional camera crews, I took my career suicide one step further. I quit my full-time staff position and accepted a six-month contract with NBC. What I had left the Peacock to pursue in the first place was suddenly a valued skill. That's because the Pentagon was going to embed reporters with military units, but they need to be relatively self-contained and light on their feet equipment-wise. I was perfect: cheap, portable, and hungry.

This period was to be the highlight of my career as a professional television journalist:

[http://youtu.be/drrdJu7dvFU]

I had the opportunity to show the network that my passion for inexpensive digital technology could produce a new kind of narrative, and a great diversity of stories. I went live several hundred times for MSNBC from around the Middle East during Operation Iraqi Freedom and in its aftermath. I used a portable satellite phone and a $3500 camera. I filed stories for MSNBC.com about the last Jew in Damascus, the benevolence of Hezbollah in a town in southern Lebanon, and Jewish emigrants who decided to live with their Bedouin Arab friends in the Negev desert. I populated my personal website with images and essays, regaling friends and family with tales of adventure and the insight of an eyewitness to history. I responded to every viewer's e-mail that I received, no matter how vitriolic (I knew I was doing well when both Arab and Jew accused me of bias). And I helped prove that this technology could produce, authoritative, credible stories for a capital-intensive medium that until now, had demanded a high price for access, with its multi-million dollar satellite systems, computer infrastructure and professional, large cameras.

As President Bush would declare from the deck of the U.S.S. Abraham Lincoln (where I had my first wartime embed), "Mission Accomplished." Except that despite NBC's promises to send me out again after I had taken a much-needed break back home in Canada -- they never did. Instead, they would hire a friend of mine who was also pioneering the use of these new technologies in broadcast TV, to essentially perform the same kind of work. As they continued to test the waters of amateur technology with others, I would be forced to take one final, dangerous freelance assignment with the network in Baghdad in 2004. By doing so, I would return to my former position as a producer, to support Tom Brokaw's pre-retirement tour through the world's hotspots. I would grit my teeth until I emerged safely outside of Iraqi airspace. That assignment would be the last time I would ever have any contact with network management. Amazingly enough however, it would not be the last time that my work would be shown on a broadcast network.

2. We Need a New Narrative

I know that it's not very "academic" of me to begin this treatise with a personal account. But what I just shared goes to the very heart of my premise: that technology's impact on traditional communication models demands a new narrative; that storytelling can be authoritative and credible; that the notion of a finished, polished message tailored to a targeted audience should no longer be a communicator's paramount undertaking; that one (increasingly endangered) foreign correspondent backed by a powerful, heavily-capitalized conglomerate is not as important as what an engaged, entrepreneurial individual might accomplish with access to the same powerful production and distribution tools for a fraction of what they cost broadcast networks and newspapers. I also speak from deep, personal experience when I share my observations of the profound transformations that have occurred in media, and they necessitate an entirely new set of rules of engagement.

3. Message: The Old Rules of Engagement

Here's a scenario that requires every ounce of an individual's persuasive powers to succeed: a homeless person begging for charity. Let's view it first through the optic of the 20th century persuasion-through-communication model.

GOAL: A financial donation.

MESSAGE: I lost my job, my home. I'm hungry. Please help me.

MEDIUM: A woman holding a sign; block letters written with a heavy black marker on a piece of cardboard.

TARGET AUDIENCE: Drivers that traffic a notoriously stop-and-go thoroughfare in an upscale part of town. It's especially busy during rush hour.

You just happen to be a member of the target audience in this instance. You usually give generously to known, trustworthy charitable institutions. If this person were part of one of those organization's campaigns, you would not have hesitated to donate. Had that been the case, you know that the individual would have been vetted by this brand-name charity, facilitating the decision-making process. The message may have been similar, but it would have been transmitted through a significantly more credible medium (a charity's communications channel).

But right here and right now, neither institutional credibility -- nor prior relationship -- will help you make a decision. Yes, you could wait to make a donation to the appropriate charity once you get to the office. But will you remember? And would that give you the same satisfaction that you would derive directly by handing a couple of dollar bills to someone so apparently in need, right here, right now?

Unnervingly, you are left to your own critical devices. Now you must judge for yourself, asking some uncomfortable questions. You evaluate the medium. Are her clothes dirty? Are they warm enough to insulate her from that impending cold front you just hear about on the radio? How old are her shoes? Does she look like she's been well fed? How old is her sign? Does the handwriting hint at some sort of education that would imply an unforeseen fall from grace?

And then there's her message. Is she really unemployed? Does she really live on the street? Does she really need help? Why should you trust the veracity of her sign?

It's all a complicated, somewhat emotional thought process that presages possible interaction with the homeless individual. Today, not only is it an unfortunate, all-too-common social occurrence, but it's also – metaphorically – an increasingly common dilemma that we all face in today's information marketplace.

In the past, information was scarce, and we could rely on a finite number of institutional filters to determine what communication should grab our attention and possibly catalyze our participation. As members of a particular audience, we were passive targets of those polished, self-contained "messages" that required nothing of us other than to stand dumbly and receive their impact if the sender's aim was true. Message, medium, target audience – was an almost mindless formula that worked with militaristic precision (I visualize a shiny, flawless torpedo speeding towards a vessel lollygagging in the middle of the sea) for so long.

But now, the barriers to entry to the Information Age have disintegrated. Almost everyone can use cheap, nearly ubiquitous technologies to communicate well beyond their immediate social circle of friends, family and co-workers. Today, we have the power to talk to the world, and the world can talk back. Information is no longer scarce – thanks to the Internet; it's more abundant than it ever has been in the history of our species. That sublimely aimed torpedo is now scattershot machine gun fire; endless ammunition squeezed off

by hundreds of millions of people wearing blindfolds.   We're
like three year-old children playing a first-person shooter video
game on the "Easy" setting: our resources are limitless and we
have infinite lives. And we're firing at each other!

Information may no longer be scarce, but our attention is in
shockingly short supply, given the exponential explosion in
potential sources of communication thanks to all of this
technology. How do we choose which voice to listen to, given
the cacophony out there?

Disconcertingly, we now also have the ability to interact
with someone who is publicly trying to get our attention. That's
enough to force us to roll up our windows and turn up the music
rather than engage socially with someone we've never met, but
so clearly wants something from us. If we caught each other's
eyes for the slightest of moments, are we now compelled to
follow through and pursue the relationship, no matter how
uncomfortable?

4. Story: A New Way to Engage

Such is our 21st century communications conundrum. How do we calculate the value proposition in deciding whether to accept someone's attempts to interact persuasively with us? Yes, we have access to more information than ever before. But we also have less ability to discern credibility as well – which is so crucial when we're trying to assess the start of a potential relationship.

What can determine our preferences in this messy, highly populated media universe? Simply put, it's what we have decided to trust, to ascribe credibility to, and to find relevant to our own lives. In the 20th century, this same equation was an easy one to calculate: we had a limited number of brand names -- institutional players that produced the media that we consumed because someone had decided it would appeal to our needs and tastes as a mass audience. We had very little choice otherwise. Some of those media companies began to amass considerable power as they monetized their production. They would either become monopolies or felt free to abuse our trust in them because of their growing power (or sometimes both). Unfortunately for these organizations, this happened to coincide with a massive revolution in technology, which suddenly gave us more choice and the power to refuse their expensively, highly produced offerings. Many of these companies are still around, some of them in a diminished state after taking a severe hit to their revenues, now forced to compete with newer, more efficient players in the industry, or even some that offer content for free. Today, all of these institutional organizations, start-ups, professionals, amateurs and citizen producers are asking the same question: how do we convince people to pay attention to what we're creating? More challengingly, how do we convince them to transact with our content in a way that justifies our effort?

In this highly creative new world of seemingly limitless producers and choice of content, where barriers to production are so low to permit almost anyone to share their media with anyone else, how do we convince people of this key value proposition? That if they determine what I'm trying to communicate is relevant to their interests, they may even find it as useful and beneficial as I do in producing and sharing it? That through this relationship of mutual benefit is one that will motivate me to keep producing this relevant content, and will motivate you to continue to trust me as a source of this relevant content?

For our homeless woman at that busy intersection, message, medium, target audience – it's all a crapshoot. But what if...

...you had been driving this route for years, and could identify any new activity at this particular intersection?

...this particular woman had suddenly shown up at this corner a few days ago, coinciding with a recent period of massive financial upheaval in your region (bank closures, layoffs)?

...her sign changed every day, as she revealed more details about the terrible set of circumstances that had forced her to beg at this street corner?

...some of your colleagues had also noticed her during their commute, had rolled down their windows to chat with her, learn more about her story, and even went so far as to begin an informal campaign at the office to find her food, shelter, and work?

Would that not make it easier for to decide whether you should help her? And from her perspective, would it not be easier for her to persuade people she did not know, to help her?

We're no longer talking about message, medium and target audience here. There are too many other dynamic factors in play for that to make much sense any more. Rather, we now have to account for context, narrative, and trusted relationships within communities (as opposed to trust in institutions) to effect the same persuasion calculation that was once so simple. Put succinctly, we now have to listen to each other's stories. This seemingly facile conclusion not only upends our traditional business communication strategies, but also affords each one of us a persuasive power that until now was the exclusive preserve of highly resourced companies and governments.

5. The Uprising

Mahatma Gandhi once said about dictatorship: "There have been tyrants...and for a time they can seem invincible, but in the end they always fall." They fall, because their injustice inspires a narrative replete with conflict that compels us to take action and restore equilibrium. That narrative was once the preserve of power leaders or powerful books. Abraham Lincoln reportedly said of the author of *Uncle Tom's Cabin* -- a novel about slavery that inspired the abolitionist movement -- "so that's the little lady who wrote the great book that started this great war".

Now powerful ideas can readily emanate from highly accessible conduits of communication, such as the dramatic murder of a political activist on the streets of Teheran, filmed on a cellphone camera, spread quickly and authoritatively among us all, by us all (the anonymously filmed, graphic *Neda* video won the George Polk Award for special achievement in journalism in 2010):

[http://youtu.be/bbdEf0QRsLM]

This is a significant enough development to merit being called an "Uprising." It's a strategy that facilitates continual, credible communication between teller and listener -- through memorable emotional narrative, enabled by the connective power of relationship and highly accessible digital technology.

Stories? Really? Aren't those relegated to bedtime, "once upon a time" and Hollywood? What do they have to do with professionals attempting to communicate persuasively?

We may still have a 20th century understanding of what "stories" are because the technologies of mass communication relegated them to Disney and "once upon a time." Within that mindset, stories are seen as pure narrative, nothing more.

Prior to the digital revolution, we had relatively few media producers, who created a common-denominator message that would be created, scripted, set, polished and distributed to a passive, mass audience who would then consume it. Think of the tens of millions of people who watched The Beatles' first appearance on the Ed Sullivan -- a musical group selected by a small number of producers to be shared with a huge audience via a powerful, expensive broadcast medium. In that world, we had to carefully consider the concepts of target audience, message segmentation and consumption.

It was an era of few producers and many (i.e. millions) of consumers. That was the Audience Equation: honed by decades of industrialized communication culture, where barriers to entry were set high by the astronomical cost of printing presses, broadcast technology, and the human resources to operate them. If you were going to spend the time and money to reach people using mass media, you had to assure yourself that you could guarantee a substantial degree of attention, which would then lead to substantial advertising revenues (or in the eyes of state-run outlets, satisfy a major public policy objective). This drove the need to filter the message prior to publication. Stories in the traditional sense were merely source material for mass media's finished output: primarily books, films and TV shows. Beyond this industrial production of story, we the audience merely told tales amongst ourselves, at bedtime, at the dinner table, in our town halls and at our places of worship.

But in the last decade, the explosion of broadband access to the Internet, powerful computer processors, cheap digital storage, and the proliferation of portable devices that help create, transmit and receive, have all thrown this very controlled communication system into turmoil. Suddenly, almost anyone (regardless of technical skill, or even economic status) can have some sort of access to a cheap, easy-to-use communication medium. So why should we bother to spend months or even years to craft a "message" when we can communicate so easily to people we hardly know -- if at all -- with the press of a key and the touch on a screen? Suddenly, we have access to what seems like an infinite amount of information, and a limitless diversity of voices and minds. Why trouble ourselves to "target" any "audience" in this environment when the cost to do so is so minimal? Indeed, audiences no longer sit passively in their seats and politely applaud (or boo, or switch the channel) as their only forms of interaction. Today, they talk back and create their own content. Often, what attracts us most to this non-traditional form of content is either its novelty or the story being conveyed.

In this new environment, storytelling isn't merely the transmission of compelling narrative. It's also about how we engage with that narrative. In many ways, how the community interacts with that narrative is ultimately what renders this form of communication trusted and persuasive. This is storytelling for the 21st century: the two-part process of structured narrative (which draws our attention) matched with a strategy of community engagement to build trusted relationships around that story. When we successfully create these new relationships, we build "social capital" and create the conditions for trust that persuade others to transact with us: change your mind, join us, vote for me, buy our product. So forget about "what's your message?" Rather, ask "what story do you want to tell?"

6. Why Stories?

In the most primordial way, we humans have been
conditioned to pay attention to stories that help us make sense
of our own lives, to which we can relate both individually, and
in a collective way. Famed mythologist Joseph Campbell
would tell us that's why our most resilient, age-old cultural
stories share such universal themes: of birth, growth,
transformation, and of death.

It sounds like an insulting resolution to an incredibly
difficult question. We've abandoned the notion of storytelling
to that quaint "once upon a time" bedtime activity, primarily
because of how communication was industrialized over the last
century and a half, with the advent of radio, television and the
film industry. We left stories to these major companies -- at
least the stories that we would share publicly and adopt as part
of our cultural conversation. We forgot that prior to the advent
of mass media and mass audiences, storytelling was much more
than a Hollywood movie.

Child psychologist Daniel Siegel says we have a
fundamental need for those stories – bedtime or not – from an
early age. "Storytelling is fundamental to all human cultures,
and our shared stories create a connection to others that builds a

sense of belonging to a particular community," Siegel wrote in
Parenting from the Inside Out (Tarcher, 2004).   That's because
we help make sense of our lives through a neurological
blending of our left (rational) and right (social and emotional)
sides of our brain. "Mental well-being may depend in many
ways upon the layers of integration that deepen our sense of
connection to ourselves and to others." In other words, stories
are good for us, and good for cohesive community. And digital
technology as an effective communication enabler allows us to
use storytelling once again to facilitate this interpersonal
integration.

7. Folk Culture Returns

Media distribution technology developed rapidly from the 19th century, with improvements to the printing press that allowed newspapers to reach even larger readerships. Radio and television soon followed facilitating long-distance access to new audiences. But the exponentially increasing cost of these new technologies required access to large numbers of people to amortize the financial investment. With the explosion of mass media outlets, came the need to appeal to mass audiences -- in a way that was universal, uniform, and antiseptic – to transcend special interests of any particular demographic. By pushing through geographic boundaries in search of common denominator consumption for media, this new form of production quickly marginalized other forms of expression shared directly within smaller communities.

This traditional "folk culture" brought storyteller and audience much closer together, literally, in the same hall, church, room or around the same fire. Storyteller and listener were more likely than not, members of the same community, capable of direct interaction with each other, facilitating near-instant feedback. This physical and social proximity also required a certain level of accountability from the storyteller. If

I wanted to be successful in my endeavor, I had to have a pretty good idea of what would resonate within the community. And in performing the actual act of telling the story (or in singing the song, acting out the drama), I would want to take cues from those in attendance, paying close attention to those moments of connection – even adapting my content to their needs as I drew them even deeper into my narrative.

Through this relationship of connected accountability, I would hope that not only would the community pay attention to what I was communicating this time, but they might be encouraged to do so the next time I had a story to tell. They had already taken a risk to invest time and attention in my story; I had structured it and filled it with sufficient content in a way that compelled them to continue to listen, ideally ensuring that their investment paid off and that their trust in this eventual pay-off was not unfounded.

This storytelling formula is a demanding calculation, fraught with challenges for the storyteller. Implicit within it is some form of "Return On Investment" for the audience (Time x Attention = Relevant Content) and for the storyteller (Creation x Distribution = Engaged Community).

It also requires something more than the "build it and they will come" Utopian view of digital media – that we're all now media outlets now, and that someone is always interested in our output. Not only is this not the case, it is also not realistic.

8. A Need for Attention

Unless our intentions are purely artistic (creating content for our own creative satisfaction with complete disregard for a desire to have anyone else look at it) our motivation to create media involves some sort of need to have others pay attention to it. Let's also assume that these are people that would not normally pay attention to anything we say or do. That's most likely because they hardly know us, if at all, without any direct contact to us other than through a technological distribution platform. So we have so-called "weak ties" to these people, which we find more inspiring because it means that we're able to convince people who have no compulsion to otherwise like what we do, that our content has value.

Isn't this the heart of communication itself? That we seek to create a relationship of information exchange requiring something more than an individual act performed in a vacuum where only we are aware of the utterance we have made?

Let's assume that one of the originating platforms of folk culture – storytelling – demands a truthful, credible relationship of mutual benefit. These relationships – with other enthusiasts, with organizations, and even with other media outlets – can help build a constellation (smaller outlets orbiting around her larger world) of influence and trust, leading to a satisfactory Return on Investment (commonly referred to as "ROI").

I believe in all of this because after I flew out of Baghdad that hot day in July 2004, I decided to try this model out for myself.

9. Independence through *Independent America*

At the same time that I was experiencing my final fit of network news desperation in Iraq, I was also pursuing other ideas.

One of them included understanding the growing phenomenon of the democratization of communication and production through digital technology. I thought we should explore this through a university-housed digital media center where I lived in rural British Columbia. I firmly believed that more accessible digital technology, combined with network access was going to produce an explosion in new voices. I contended that we needed to study this phenomenon and prepare ourselves for its consequences, hopefully taking advantage of the inevitable social and economic impact.

At the same time, I began to realize that as I settled into my life in a far-flung region of North America, I was befriending a good number of retail owners in the area. As I was quickly cutting my attachment to the broadcast networks, their entrepreneurial mission inspired me. I also noticed the growing proliferation of big box chain stores around town, and when we'd drive south to see my in-laws in Seattle. I had clearly missed out on a lot during my nearly four years in the Middle East. I found these behemoths profoundly alienating. I would fall into a deep, frustrated funk anytime I had to scavenge through a cavernous Home Depot. I worried about my new friends, and wondered if they were nothing but the dying gasp of mythical Mom & Pop.

To recover my from my six-month Middle East tour of duty, and to reacquaint ourselves, my wife and I took a trip down the historic Pacific Coast Highway, from Seattle to San Luis Obispo. For fun, we vowed not to rely on the Interstate, and not to do business with any corporate chains. I ended up shooting a short film of our journey, and writing about it for MSNBC.com. I liked what we had discovered, and set on a path to find a broadcaster to support a national road trip to document this new retail reality. At the same time, a grassroots "Buy Local" organization in Montana had posted my article to their website. I thanked its founders directly for doing so.

I relished the idea of pursuing both the digital media center and documentary projects, and reached out to major players who might support each. I spoke to higher-ups from IBM, the University of British Columbia, I attended Canadian Parliament in Ottawa so I could meet the Commerce Minister, I flew to Washington D.C. as a finalist for funding with the Corporation for Public Broadcasting. But I failed to convince anyone to provide the seed money we needed to go ahead with either venture.

My final tour in Iraq had helped replenish our bank account, and I had also experimented with blogging while I was overseas. Upon my return, I met up with someone my father had met at an event in Toronto who was also looking to get into documentary film production. He had access to a small amount of funding, but didn't have any solid distribution or broadcast leads for us. Tom Powers liked our documentary pitch, and wanted to partner with us. I had to consider the myriad ways I had shot myself in the foot professionally over the last few years because of my need to explore, to be one step ahead, to pursue a more authentic and satisfying career reality for myself. This huge sacrifice had merely resulted in me finding myself with my back against the wall, armed with two decent ideas that weren't resonating with too many other people.

So I decided to do what anyone else in a no-win situation would do: I doubled down and rolled the dice. I decided to take Tom's offer – along with some assistance from my family -- and I would prove that both ideas had value – by creating a film through the democratized tools of media production that I was championing through a digital media center.

And so it was, in the first quarter of 2005, as blogging began to take off, high definition video had just descended to consumer-level prices, and starts-ups were beginning to introduce online distribution platforms for multimedia (YouTube would launch later that year), that we created *Independent America: The Two-Lane Search for Mom & Pop.* [http://www.hulu.com/watch/105821/independent-america or http://vimeo.com/hrhmedia/independentamerica]

It would be a story that we would tell and share through digital media, leading to an ROI of broadcast and DVD sales, homepage features on Yahoo!, Hulu and Snagfilms, activist influence, and ultimately a job as the Director of the Master of Communication in Digital Media at the University of Washington in Seattle.

10. The Story I Wanted to Tell

In this age of successful films such as *Julie and Julia*, what I'm about to explain may not sound especially groundbreaking. But as much as a Hollywood blockbuster can illuminate the way forward for showcasing new stories, so can a niche success like *Independent America*.

I'll spare you suspense. Here's what I'm getting at. In this digital age of democratized production and cheap distribution, you need to tell stories like it's 1599. Okay, that's a little too glib and folk culture-centric, but strategically include 21st century social media tools, and that's all you need. Tell stories, build community, and find your ROI.

Once we had found minimal financial support through our new partner Tom, to produce a homemade film, we faced two elemental production challenges. What was going to make for a compelling sixty-plus minute documentary? And without the credibility and institutional backing of a powerful organization (such as NBC), why would anyone want to talk to us? This was very much my to-be-expected traditional media fear as a professional. If I didn't have a broadcaster, why would anyone want to participate in, or support, the film? If no one participated in, or was not interested in supporting, the film, why would anyone want to broadcast it?   And of course: what was my message? Who was my audience?

When I originally proposed a film that would follow a married couple and their dog (somewhat inspired by the books *Blue Highways*, *My Travels with Charley*, and *On the Road*) who would travel across America without availing themselves of interstates or corporate chain retail, I initially saw these two constraints as the headline "gimmick." I believed the real story to be a hard-hitting look at how Mom & Pop retailers were about to disappear because of an uneven playing field that favored big box stores. I would only figure out later that the constraints themselves were the story. In retrospect, I recall the off-air comments of a local NPR radio host in Fayetteville, Arkansas who had just finished interviewing us (at that point, we were a third of the way through our journey). He said that we were doing something that most Americans only dreamed of doing – a cross-country adventure on America's historic by-ways, which was enough to captivate anyone's imagination. In the years that followed, Americans who had seen the film and wanted to recreate our itinerary occasionally contacted me for advice and inspiration. I would also come across a *The New York Times* article on divorce of all things, which would observe that the road trip is the quintessential American vehicle for starting anew, "a deep cultural notion that the path to renewal lies in breaking away and moving on."

So, although our reporting on the plight of various characters in far-flung parts of the country drove us to make the film, others were actually inspired by our story. More to the point, who was this married couple that faced this unique challenge, and would they succeed in their quest?

The lesson to draw here is that the "message" and "audience" question might apply when considering the creation of content within a traditional media/institutionalized model, where you ask questions first then shoot. But in my situation, only one question really mattered. What story did we want to tell? Our primary motivation was not to make a blockbuster film, but rather to satisfy our urge to tell a particular story about America. The cost of the tools to do so had dropped so precipitously that the only real expenses would be our time and travel logistics.

The primary question that remained was how to create sufficiently attractive content so that people that we didn't know would be interested in paying attention to it. The answer lay in the structure that we created through the road trip narrative.

11. The Power of Structure

Both Aristotle and Joseph Campbell might observe that we were about to embody the ideal story structure with *Independent America*.

Why is this structure so crucial? In *Poetics* Aristotle observed what we now consider to be so obvious; that every story has a "beginning, middle and end." In itself, that doesn't seem to do anything other than identify when you have a story before you, rather than a loose compendium of information.

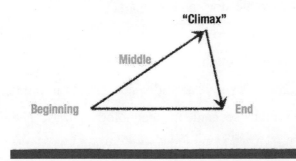

But Aristotle also likened this structure to the tightening of a knot, laying out the premise of the story at the outset, and then twisting it tighter into a "complication" until some sort of transformation occurred (the "climax"), leading to a release of the knot and the story's tension (the "denouement" – literally the untying of the complication).

Many of us may remember this beginning-middle-and-end exhortation of story structure from our days in grade school, with perhaps an unfair emphasis on the "climax" or the middle, due to the effort required in dreaming up a compelling plot (that had the appeal of the highest drama near the middle). However, as both Aristotle and Michael Tierno in *Aristotle's Poetics for Screenwriters* (Hyperion, 2002) would observe, the end is equally important. That's when we let the audience "off the hook," giving them an emotional release through conclusion. In that release comes catharsis, and a certain empathy that connects us to the story and its characters.

In Hollywood parlance, consider Luke Skywalker's dramatic flight through the trenches of the Death Star in the original *Star Wars*. We as audience were at the edge of our seats. Would he set aside his technology and use The Force? Would Darth Vader catch him first? Would he hit the target? We are in pure story climax at this stage. Just as we can't bear it any longer, and it appears as if the Empire will prevail, Hans Solo comes out of nowhere; his Millennium Falcon spaceship

triumphantly framed by a shining star, and gives Luke the
opportunity to make his successful shot. We rejoice, we breathe
again, and as we're let off the hook, we settle down and
recognize that we've been on one amazing journey as Princess
Leia hands out the medals to the heroes and Chewbacca lets out
a mighty roar. (It bears mentioning that George Lucas, the
movie's director, drew great inspiration from Joseph
Campbell's *Hero with a Thousand Faces* for the *Star Wars*
storyline).

   This emotional element is crucial: it actually helps us make
decisions. I noted earlier how child psychiatrist Dan Siegel says
that we connect to each other using the integrated hemispheres
(emotion, rational) of our brains. In *How We Decide* (Mariner
Books 2010), Jonah Lehrer says that the right side of our brain
allows us to see what we would otherwise fail to notice with our
rational hemisphere. Lehrer says, "These wise yet inexplicable
feelings are an essential part of the decision-making process.
Even when we think we know nothing, our brains know
something. That's what our feelings are trying to tell us."

   This means that if we're (a) competing for attention in an
information-saturated society, and (b) we want to encourage
people to make decisions based on our communication, the

emotional impact of a story can help us accomplish both --
overcoming these two significant 21st century challenges.

In *Independent America*, the middle would consist of the
mounting tension of whether we'd complete the journey as we
encountered challenges along the way – mirrored by bad news
for independent retailers in the small towns we were passing
through. As we reached the end of our journey, we also reached
an epiphany on the growing mistrust Americans were beginning
to exhibit for large, powerful institutions; and an increasing
need for economic self-sufficiency through neighborhood
retailers. At the same time, we discovered a positive
"homegrown" solution in a community-supported department
store, fortuitously near the end of our journey in Wyoming. Not
only do we successfully complete our quest, but we find an
answer to the question we had posed at the outset.

Aristotle would contend that this middle tension and final
release are satisfying to a story's audience – that we have
returned on their investment in attention and time, through this
emotional bond. With this new relationship of empathy, we
would now be seen as credible storytellers, and might be able to
re-engage an audience for future communication. We had
earned their attention merely by creating an effective story
structure.

But can everything we want to communicate be so easily restructured into a dramatic piece of narrative film? What if we're a non-profit organization trying to develop a new, inspiring vision statement ahead of a major fundraising campaign? Or what if we're just trying to share our resume with a potential employer? If we restructured it as a story on a bio page of our website, would that help us convey any modicum of emotion, followed by a sort of resolution that would create an empathetic bond with a potential employer? How powerful does that emotional element need to be?

In *Made to Stick* (Random House, 2007), authors Chip and Dan Heath explain how we experience curiosity when "we feel a gap in our knowledge." The authors refer to economist George Loewenstein's theory that this gap actually causes a mild form of pain. It works for stories as well when we ask questions like "What will happen?" "Who did it?" or in the case of someone's online biography, "How did this person get to this station in life?" Through this slight pain of curiosity -- and by creating a sense of urgency -- the storyteller compels us to feel for attempted communication, and by answering the question, we can scratch that itch, alleviate the pain, and fill the gap.

12. The Power of Connection

While we're looking at the instinctive, intrinsic reasons why we pay attention to stories, there's an even more primordial one: stories are encoded within our DNA as humans.

Joseph Campbell spent his life studying myths from around the world. While doing so, he came across a universal pattern that transcends both culture and history. He called it "the Hero's Journey" – when a seemingly ordinary person reluctantly accepts a call to action, leaves behind his status quo, and embarks on a journey that entails trials and tribulations from which this "hero" learns valuable lessons. Ultimately, he undergoes a form of transformation for better or for worse, and returns home a changed person. Jesus, Moses, Mohammed, Harry Potter, Frodo and yes Luke Skywalker – they all took the mythical Hero's Journey.

Yet again with Campbell, as with Aristotle, a hero's path does not need to be nearly as dramatic and profound as a biblical character or a protagonist from a fantasy trilogy. Campbell believed that our love and belief in these myths originated from our very own experiences as human beings, who are born, who live and die; that we are all pursuing our own Hero's Journey, with a clear beginning, middle and end, with a transformation along the way. We are born (call to action) as a dependent being, requiring food, shelter, clothing, discipline and education. As we grow, we reach the apex of our power as self-responsible, independent adults. Now at the peak, we begin our slow decline into old age, where we are dismissed, and then disengaged from life. We all inherently grasp this three-stage transformation deep within our very being – indeed we spend our lives trying to understand it and coming to terms with it – so it's no wonder that disparate societies can tell the very same stories over and over again (just substitute names, places and details) and yet we still find ourselves so deeply attracted to these archetypal tales.

This Hero's Journey has served as the blueprint for many who wish to overcome the challenge of communication: from Hollywood screenwriters trying to entertain audiences to educators hoping their lessons will resonate with students. Education technology expert Jason Ohler wrote in his *Digital Storytelling in the Classroom* (Corwin Press, 2007) "I have come to believe, on a very basic level that feels biological to me, that we need stories…They give communities coherence and our lives meaning…One of the most powerful stories a teacher can have students tell is the story of their future selves, in which they become heroes of the lives they want to live."

Ohler has applied Campbell's mythical structures to his own teaching, as you can see in this diagram:

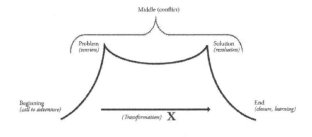

So here we are in the 21st century, struggling to understand how to break through the haze of a multiplicity of sources of information, all struggling to catch our attention and inspire us into some form of action; and here we have a timeless practice to assist us in overcoming these communication challenges.

13. Content and Community

Still, in this technologically transformed ecosystem, the actual creation and development of story is just the first step. There's another key element to storytelling – one that was so obvious before it was rendered temporarily obsolete by mass industrialized one-way media in the 20th century. Today, digital media platforms have resurrected this key component, and now allow us to ply it back into the trust equation as it relates to communication. It allows us to create community around our content.

Certainly advertisers and public relations professionals have never forgotten Campbell and Aristotle's story exhortations, telling stories in marketing campaigns, sometimes even serializing them like a television drama. But these were still very much 20th century mass media products of passive, one-way, filter-then-publish media distribution. They demanded only that we consume their finished messages, even if they were mildly dramatic, because they followed theories of story structure, standing out from the typical "this is why our product is great" superlative. This may have worked when anyone looking to co-opt the story forms was part of a large organization employing highly exclusive, expensive broadcast methods to convey these messages. We either had no choice but to sit through that commercial – or look at that ad – or we implicitly trusted what the communicator was saying by the very fact that the utterance appeared in a certain medium. In other words, we were ascribing credibility to an organization that must be trustworthy due to the huge resources and effort it deployed in its endeavor to reach us; we concluded that those high barriers to entry must count for something, winnowing out the losers and the charlatans.

But in the digital age, those barriers to entry have eroded. In many ways, they're no longer a feasible metric for credibility and trust because we're all so capable of playing in this communication space. At this stage, we're more likely to ignore the noise that envelops us than to pay it any mind. So let's retain this notion of storyteller and community – where each is the other's trusted audience. In his groundbreaking *Wealth of Networks* (Yale University Press, 2007), Yochai Benkler calls it an "unfinished conversation" between producer and user, thanks to the very social attributes of the Internet, and its many digital conveyances. Trust no longer emanates exclusively from the power of a brand name or from the overpowering resources of a recognizable institution. Thanks to the promulgation of weak ties in social networks, we have learned to trust people we may have never met, as long as we can identify some mutual interest that allows us to agree on something, encouraging us to open a channel of communication. If we inject that channel with story, authenticity, and a certain amount of emotion, we have laid the groundwork for an ongoing relationship of credible communication. This is an immensely important development in social power disbursement, which we'll address later.

This democratizing technology has also had a huge impact on the dominant control larger institutions once had over information and "message." This carries deep implications as we seek to understand our new communications ecosystem. We are increasingly engaged in social production through digital networks. Charlene Li and Josh Bernoff in *Groundswell* (Harvard Business Review Press, 2008) identified how segments of consumers are now participating in some form of online social activity. They developed a scale called "social technographics" to measure this development, from Creators, Critics, Collectors, Joiners, Spectators and Inactives. When they published the book in 2008 48% of online Americans were involved in some sort of social participation. In 2009, that number had risen to 80%, with a full 24% identified as Creators

– participants who might publish a web page, maintain a blog, or upload a video.

Amazon.com's former Chief Scientist would come out that same year and boldly declare (without revealing his methodology) that in 2009 "more data will be generated by individuals than in the entire history of mankind through 2008. Information overload is more serious than ever," ("The Social Data Revolution(s), *HBR Blog Network*, May 20, 2009)."

In a way, we may have finally rebuilt the fabled library of Alexandria – bigger, better and more interactive than ever.

When my wife and I went out to join the still intimate group of creators in 2005 to produce *Independent America*, we were lacking two key attributes that I took for granted when I worked at NBC: credibility and a distribution platform. We had a potentially great story, with no affiliation, and no obvious way to get the story out. In the last century, we would not have fathomed the idea of moving beyond that state; maybe we would have just tormented our family at the dinner table with sad stories of what could have been.

But in 2005, I realized we had a growing number of options. I had my old vanity website still up on Tripod.com:

[http://aminstrel.tripod.com/]

I had experimented with Google's Blogger while in Iraq, documenting how I kept cool under fire thanks to my reacquaintance with yoga (I still remember my less tech-savvy friends back in Canada asking my wife "what's a blog?" – a highly legitimate question back in 2004):

[http://www.hrhmedia.blogspot.com/]

And I had sold a few shares of newly resurgent Apple Computer to provide the funds so that I could be one of the first to buy Sony's new foray into prosumer high definition digital video with the HVR-Z1U camera. This tool was so new, that when we set out on our trip, neither of my video editing suites – Avid or Final Cut Pro – could handle this new compressed HD codec. I knew well enough that software revisions would come later in the year, just as we would have completed shooting the film. I just hoped that I wouldn't have to be the one who would have to wrestle with such an unwieldy, processor-intensive task like film editing. My hopes were ultimately in vain.

I also had a couple of other tools at my disposal. There was a new blogging platform called Typepad, which through another social media startup would facilitate my posting of audio and video files. This would allow me to keep a multimedia production diary as we filmed:

[http://www.independentamerica.typepad.com/]

I was very excited about this, as it would allow me to pursue what I had found least gratifying about my work in television journalism. I would be able to maintain a value-added repository for all the ideas and content we were gathering, sometimes in their rawest form. I wouldn't have to leave 90% of my work on the cutting-room floor.

Despite all this, I was still in somewhat of a mass media frame of mind. I didn't see this particular trip as the official shoot for the documentary. Rather, I was looking at it as a producers' research road trip, where we'd gather stories and clips for a full-fledged proposal for funding. We could then return the following year with a "proper" camera crew, a comfortable RV, and all the accoutrements befitting of a "big" idea. As it was with my fantasy of having someone else to edit the film, this would never happen. The journey was the story. The trip was the documentary.

The other tool at our disposal was less tangible, and certainly less technology-related. It was a nascent relationship with the grassroots organization that had originally cross-posted my MSNBC article from our Pacific Coast Highway trip in 2003. I had stayed in touch with Jennifer Rockne from the American Independent Business Alliance, all that time, declaring my undying commitment to producing a larger story

about the burgeoning Buy Local "resistance" movement.
Jennifer, in turn, would connect me with AMIBA's members
across the country, motivated to tell the story of their local
campaigns and struggles they faced. As I contemplated
documenting our ordeal on Typepad, I realized I could call upon
AMIBA to help drive their members to our blog, maybe even
providing advice along the way. This simple request for help
was why we succeeded. First, it helped shaped a good portion
of the final story. As our community grew, that began to advise
us of conflicts between Big Box stores and Mom & Pop on the
road ahead.

We even put a general call for help when we realized that if
we were shooting a film called "Independent America" we
should find an appropriate location to shoot on Independence
Day. I indicated that on July 4th, we'd be somewhere between
Indiana and Nebraska. The response from the community was
swift. Didn't I know that Seward, Nebraska, near Lincoln, was
the Small Town July 4th capital of the United States? And if
that wasn't already perfect enough, the family that organized
the annual festivities was staunchly Republican, who harbored
strong reservations about the disruptive economic clout of the
newly established Wal-Mart superstore on their town's outskirts
(there wasn't a single chain store on Seward's Main Street and

most residents like it that way – they wanted to continue doing business with their neighbors).

By engaging our online community members, we would also build a large amount of social capital with them. Before the end of the trip, they would trust our influential observations so much, that they would start to pressure us to transfer the film to DVD as soon as possible. They wanted to buy it so they could screen it in their communities, hoping to convince neighbors and city officials that they had to reform economic policy as it related to retail.

14. Trust and Social Capital

So why did this work? First, the structure of our narrative made our content in itself inherently compelling to a particular group of people.

Then, our approach to producing the film, by sharing the process and our findings along the way through our blog with a small, passionate community, allowed us to build "social capital" within a network. In other words, by reaching out to a particular community, we managed to establish trust that led to a certain degree of reciprocity.

This rebuts the famous "Prisoners' Dilemma" thought experiment. New York University Professor Clay Shirky explores this further in his *Here Comes Everybody* (Penguin Books, 2008). Under the classic scenario, two people are accused of conspiring to commit a crime. They're put into separate jail cells for questioning. The police tell each one of them that they can go free if they turn the other in. Assuming that the prisoners can't communicate with each other, nor do they trust each other, the most likely outcome is that each will turn the other in, and they're both charged.

The best scenario would be that neither speaks, and they're both set free for lack of evidence. Due to that lack of communication and trust, that's not likely.   But what if there were a way for the prisoners to interact, and see what the other was doing? What if Prisoner A said nothing to the police, Prisoner B saw this trust-building gesture, and did the same? In a way, the original Prisoners' Dilemma is akin to the world of passive, mass media where there is little to no communication between audience and the media organization. But in a more interactive ecosystem, the more storytellers share with their community (in that great "unfinished conversation"), the more trust is created.

In *Foundations of Social Theory* (Belknap Press, 1998) sociological theorist James Coleman identified four elements of what constitutes trustworthy behavior, and what it might lead to:

(1) The decision to ascribe trust facilitates an act that would not otherwise be possible (in our case, ascribing credibility to a pair of unknown, amateur filmmakers).

(2) The person placing that trust (the "trustor"), will be better off for placing that trust in the stranger (the "trustee").

(3) Trust itself is an act that entails a voluntary transfer of resources (be they physical, financial, intellectual or temporal) from the trustor to the trustee. Here, Coleman says there is no real commitment from the trustee (identifying the classic

Prisoner's Dilemma). But in our new social storytelling ecosystem, we the trustees were also making a commitment to the trustor – that we would listen, and even modify the nature of our relationship based on valuable inputs from the trustor. In other words, we would see this as a 2-way relationship, also known as *Wealth of Networks'* Benkler's "unfinished conversation."

(4) There's usually a time lag between the extension of trust and the ensuing trusting behavior.

Trust in this informal, spontaneous community is key, as philosopher Francis Fukuyama said; the community would not arise without it.

Once a community is established, its effectiveness and cohesiveness can potentially be measured by two elements: the degree to which it is held together, and the extent to which it can be extended to other people beyond the original community.

Another way of looking at this is in terms of "capital" that we can create to sustain and grow it. Sociologists would say that it's easier to create "bonding" capital – building ties that link people together with others who are primarily like them in some key manner. Our reaching out to AMIBA with a film concept that implicitly celebrated independent retailers, and sought to "expose" corporate chain dominance would find a welcome audience within the organization's membership. So our editorial premise facilitated the creation of this bonding capital. What would prove to be more challenging would be our attempt to move beyond this potential "echo chamber" of like-minded community members, and reach out further to groups that typically might not find much in common with our ideas (or would be primarily uninspired to even seek out a film like ours). Should we succeed, this would take our creation outside of a niche community, to a larger audience, allowing us to potentially change a good number of people's minds about how they shopped and supported their local economies.

On one hand, there's power in appealing to that niche community that may have the passion and focus to support a fairly narrow, non-mainstream idea such as *Independent America*. Even more particular, was that we had deliberately abandoned the mass media era veneer of journalistic objectivity (a highly industrialized blunting of the editorial edges to appeal to a large, mass audience without offending them), which would further relegate us to the populist sidelines. But the power of networks might allow us to sustain our project through this narrow community if they bought enough DVD's and told enough of their friends about the film. Social media via a series of social bonding transactions would be enough to form such a community.

But how could we bridge social groups and create that other kind of capital that would allow us to reach beyond the converted and true believers? Would social media such as blogs and podcasts be enough? Or would our bonded adherents "tell two friends" who might be as like-minded as they were, unable to convert non-believers to the cause?

To a certain extent, this would require the "power of story" to make a convincing case for itself to bring the undecided or the Wal-Mart enthusiast on board. We were not particularly objective, but we were fair, and not dogmatic in our approach to the film and in our conclusions. We made our editorial practices transparently clear in our blog, through our mission statement and our posts. We would also link to sites that did not make our most ardent supporters happy, such as Wal-Mart Facts.com. We thought it was the fair thing to do. Ultimately, this practice would convince the Wal-Mart executive communications team, which receives 800 interview requests a week, to cooperate with us, a no-name film production team that didn't even have a distributor. But we had begun to build a community, we had begun to share our content for the world to see, and we had made our position as transparent as we could.

Some might say this made our mission and our "message" authentic.

Would that be enough to appeal to non-enthusiasts? We had convinced Wal-Mart to at least cooperate with us, even if we didn't see eye to eye. Maybe our bonded enthusiasts who had asked us to sell them the DVD would host community screenings with the hope of effecting a change in attitudes and policy through what we hoped was a powerful, entertaining story. It would also be up to us to reach out to non-like minded communities to convince them we could be trusted.

By doing so, we were able to break out of our narrow community to a much broader-based one by connecting to a diversity of communications streams. The blog itself was a good start, but we also needed journalists, who still had access to more diverse "mass audiences." Newspaper articles and radio interviews along the way helped achieve this. As we secured broadcasters around the world, their still influential reach brought us new communities who were interested in what we had to say, and how we were saying it. And larger online media outlets such as ABCNews.com, BusinessWeek.com made our content immensely sharable, especially when we made it to the big time, when Yahoo! News serialized parts of the film over two weeks.

You might find it ironic that someone who had championed non-mass media strategies and tools would resort to such a hypocritical public distribution strategy. But the very nature of how we form our networks may demand a tactical approach to this newly formed communication ecosystem. We needed to break out beyond our relatively small number of dedicated supporters – which could sustain our film for only so long. We had to harbor a more open-minded approach to building community at the distribution stage.

At this point, it's crucial to grasp the fundamental distinction between bonding and bridging capital, why we started with one, and had to move to the other. It also makes the case for the need for a "sweet spot" – somewhere between the monopolistic, hierarchic and centralized mass media outlets of the 20th century and the atomistic, anarchic and decentralized nature of citizen production and distribution; between institution and amateur; between left and right brain. At that sweet spot lie influential media creators who may be entrepreneurially minded professionals and organizations that can now serve as trusted conduits of information within specific communities. They can build this sustained influence through the emotional connectivity and interactivity of storytelling.

This potentially runs counter to the utopian view of digital media, where the power is in the network and every citizen wants to participate in a higher form of interactive communication. *Groundswell*'s Social Technographic scale aside, this isn't always the case, even among the most technologically adept of us. We still need the filter; we still need sources we can rely upon for professionalism and trust when we opt not to actively involve ourselves in the two-way relationship of communication.

A counterpoint to our active participation in storytelling would be our facility to listen and interpret the media that we'd rather more passively consume. This requires critical thinking, and an ability to ascertain whether we can trust the source. In this world of millions of media outlets that continue to emerge, we have an obligation to behave as a reporter might – taking in information from one source, and then corroborating it through several others before reaching the conclusion to trust it, and then even act upon it.

Public relations firm Edelman's Steve Rubel would say that Americans, faced "with infinite choices, powerful search tools and equally helpful friends" are changing how they consume information. It's a wonderful new world, with considerably less loyalty to the traditional "general interest" sources. But it also demands more effort from us. We simply cannot trust the first utterance of an idea, especially one that might seem initially far-fetched. In fact, Edelman, publishes an annual "Trust Barometer" report. In 2009, it concluded that we now have to hear something three to five times before we will believe it.

So, for instance, if I read on Twitter that a plane has landed on the Hudson River, I won't trust this to be true immediately. However, because this information comes to me from a person in my network to whom I have already ascribed some credibility (by the simple act of my choosing to follow them, even if I have never met this person), will I actually bother to take the next step to verify the incident? I might check with other friends online, call someone, turn on the TV or the radio, or check in on a more influential website with broader social capital than I possess.

That said, my network may trump all of this if suddenly, a photograph shows up, snapped by a witness on their cellphone camera, beamed instantly to the world thanks to the communicative power of that person's social network, and his socially-motivated desire to tell a story.

In the *Storyteller Uprising* world, the "sweet spot" approach helps us communicate to others who seek to make sense of all this information, ascribe trust, and determine the actions they take based on the information. It leaves less of a role for institutional legacy media to play, but they've already fallen somewhat into disrepute. More entrepreneurially minded storytellers who reach out directly to communities to form relationships of trust can now serve as the primary information conduit.

15. Story Inspires Action

I'm frequently asked, "What's the next Facebook or Twitter?

This query belies a sense of unease over the permanence of these tools. It also exhibits some trepidation about being left behind if we're not already "in the know" about the latest social network. That is, if we're not in the right place at the right time on the social web, we're missing the opportunity to connect with those who matter.

But what if I say, "It really doesn't matter?"

All of these social media platforms are merely "enablers," "accelerants," or as Facebook founder Mark Zuckerberg likes to qualify his own site, "utilities." They are conduits of the vital content that affords us the ability to make those relevant, relational connections.

Content. Not conversation. For sure, much of what moves through the second-by-second data stream that is the social web is primarily chatter (often inane) – the equivalent to what we might have relegated to a phone call or hastily scribbled note a few years previous. There is some power in keeping these lines of communication open, especially as we've moved away from mainly one-to-one conversations in our private lives to many-to-many (I use my cellphone primarily for online communication rather than to make calls). But when we move beyond this chatter to a URL that transports the user to the sharing of superlative content – or an excellent story – and sparks can fly.

What's a good example of this conversion of story to action?

In early 2011, a debate raged among the giants of those who study media (including the *New Yorker*'s Malcolm Gladwell and NYU's Clay Shirky) on whether the "Arab spring" – the citizen-generated uprisings throughout the Middle East that saw regimes in Tunisia and Egypt topple – would have occurred had it not been for online social networking.

A fragile cease-fire settled in among these thought leaders as they agreed that there probably would have still been revolution regardless of accessibility to the technology. They also generally conceded that perhaps its scale and speed were greatly facilitated by the easy availability of social technologies such as Facebook on YouTube -- tapping into an already burgeoning level of discontent.

Certainly, social media alerted unhappy citizens to the fact that they were not alone. As they discovered other like-minded conspirators, they could self-organize to take some sort of action against the regime. But it is the *nature* of that action that matters most in this case. All the Facebook "Likes" in the world related to some posted anti-regime diatribe would never strike sufficient fear in the heart of a dictator to compel him to abdicate.

Communication is cheap, and increasingly, its consequences are devalued as it becomes so easy to register our thoughts and opinions on a particular matter. As Malcolm Gladwell pointed out in his often-quoted October 2010 *New Yorker* article, "Small Change," engaging in such online activity doesn't ask too much of them. This minimizes the power of their commitment, and by extension, the lasting consequences of their actions to actually produce systemic change.

But if citizens put themselves in peril – thereby raising the stakes, and the value of their action – by, say, confronting the state's manifestation of physical coercion that protects political power (the police, the army), then this kind of systemic change is more likely. (Criticism of Gladwell's original piece included that when you reside in an authoritarian state where the Internet is regulated and under police surveillance, there's very real peril in the very same online activities that we consider low-stake in the democratic world).

Yes, social technologies connect people in ways that allow them to congregate and share ideas in great numbers. And that sense of movement and momentum can actually give them the fortitude to take to the streets, and raise the stakes by increasing the value of their ideas through physical, potentially dangerous action. But what really inspires that inciting action, to seek others out, and to ultimately go public and declare their convictions to the world?

These particular "uprisings" began, in my view, quite clearly with a story:

The protests that began this past January in Tunisia had nothing to do with any of this. They started when a struggling street vendor in that country's desolate heartland publicly set himself on fire after a local officer cited his cart for a municipal violation. His frustration, multiplied hundreds of thousands times, boiled over in a month of demonstrations against Tunisian President Zine al-Abidine Ben Ali. To the amazement of the Arab world, Mr. Ben Ali fled the country when the military declined to back him by brutally putting down the demonstrations.

Spurred on by televised images and YouTube videos from Tunisia, protests broke out across much of the rest of the Arab world. Within weeks, millions were on the streets in Egypt and Hosni Mubarak was gone, shown the door in part by his longtime backer, the U.S. government. The Obama administration was captivated by this spontaneous outbreak of democratic demands and at first welcomed it with few reservations (*The Wall Street Journal*, "The New Cold War," April 16, 2011).

The self-immolation of Mohamed Bouazizi, the "struggling street vendor" mentioned in the above *The Wall Street Journal* feature was the emotional trigger for Tunisians. This terrible, dramatic act helped them finally realize that the systemic corruption and oppression that they had lived with for so long was no longer tolerable. The success of their uprising, transmitted around the world through compelling visuals on YouTube and Al-Jazeera TV set fire to a similar, seething movement in Egypt (already simmering after the death of a young blogger at the hands of Egyptian police in Alexandria).

These stories inspired feelings and the creation of communities of activists/revolutionaries who took concrete, forceful, perilous actions on the streets of these two countries, and then later, throughout the region. In his *The Digital Origins of Dictatorship and Democracy* (Oxford University Press, 2010) my University of Washington colleague Dr. Phil Howard, concurs that the impact of information technologies have helped to advance democratic practices when deployed in societies ripe for change (especially those with well-educated, "wired" populations). But even when the Egyptian government shut off the nation's access to the Internet, the calls to action – and the protests – continued. Howard explained in an interview that is citizens' own personal stories of oppression that helped them relate to the larger movement.

"What actually gets someone to go onto the street to face tear gas or rubber bullets is not a piece of propaganda, but it's a picture of a mother or daughter, brother or father, who's been beaten by the police," he said ("Social media playing role in Egypt, Tunisia protests," *KING5 News*, January 26, 2011).

16. The Action Idea

In *Aristotle's Poetics for Screenwriters*, Michael Tierno calls Aristotle's focus on action in stories "fanatical." This is not the modern day "action" that we might see in a Hollywood blockbuster car chase scene. Rather, Tierno points out it's "about action that is larger than life itself and greater than the person who partakes in it." In many ways, it's the kind of action that inspires historic shifts like the Arab spring.

Tierno transposes Aristotle further into the 21st century by introducing the concept of the *Action-Idea* – in essence, the mission statement of a story. For him, this summary (usually no more than a paragraph or two) should be sufficient to "move listeners who merely hear it," powerful enough "so that when it's expanded into a film, a screenplay, whatever, it will hold and move an audience."

The Action-Idea must not only be the launching point for the development of the actual story, it must also serve as the story's singular path of alignment, with clear beginning, middle and end with an "Action" that sets the plot in motion (Joseph Campbell would call this the Hero's "Call to Action"). It's always a reminder that we should never stray too far from our story's central purpose. By creating this alignment, we strike at the essence of what it is we seek to communicate.

Tierno identifies several Action-Ideas in relation to well-known Hollywood films in *Poetics for Screenwriters.* Here's one:

After an attempt on Don Corleone's life, Michael, who has forsaken the family Mafia business, kills Sollozzo and Police Captain McCluskey to save his family, then takes over the family business, kills all his rivals, soon rises to the top of the American Mafia, and becomes the new Godfather. He then kills all the enemies he has <u>inside</u> his family. His fate as Godfather is sealed.

The Action-Idea to *The Godfather* is a powerful one – clearly delineating a beginning, middle (conflict, transformation) – and wholeheartedly memorable. It's succinct, relatable and in some ways universal in its mission. Obviously, we probably can't imagine ourselves as murderous crime syndicate bosses. But pull the lens back a bit further and this is nothing more than a story about a protagonist who resists the lure to follow in his father's footsteps, but ultimately is forced to do so.

Yes, it's a fun exercise for movies that we cherish, but what if we applied this concept to the Arab spring?

Frustrated by corrupt government officials that deny him a business permit and publicly humiliate him, a young man sets himself on fire in the center of town. Enraged by his death, citizens take to the streets and force the overthrow of their government. This sets off a chain reaction throughout the region as people of other nations come to understand that they now have the power to effect regime change.

If someone aspired to producing a documentary that encapsulated this historic point in time in the Middle East, this particular Action-Idea would serve as a helpful roadmap to guide the project's storyline.

Tierno, Campbell, and Aristotle all focus on the story's power through the universal draw of emotion through narrative. But that's only half of its allure as a communication strategy. Recall what child psychologist Daniel Siegel observed, "Our shared stories create a connection to others that builds a sense of belonging to a particular community." With that "sense of belonging" comes a growing feeling of trust among a group of people, which can catalyze a sale, a vote, or outright upheaval in a nation's political system.

This is the second stage of the communication equation that as I indicated earlier, has become so important in the digital age: once you've gotten someone's *attention*, you then need to inspire a sustainable robust level of *engagement* that leads to the desired transaction that compelled you to initiate the communication in the first place. Getting to engagement begins with establishing a sufficient level of trust.

To illustrate how story builds trust, I often run an exercise among a group of people who barely know each other. Here's what I ask them to do:

(1) Create a 1-minute (maximum) oral presentation that tells your story (or your organization's).

(2) Do so through an Action-Idea with a beginning, middle and end. It can be a particular episode, or a life story.

(3) Stand up and share your story (no need to memorize, you can read it from a sheet of paper, but please do so with some "verbal passion") with the group.

Even after only the first couple of stories is shared in that roomful of strangers, I always sense a shift in energy. It's almost as if a "thickening' occurs among the participants as they begin to understand each other a little more, and even develop a sense of trust as they partake in this creative, sometimes painful exercise. As one of my storytelling students once observed, "We've become a particular community as we have shared our stories and now feel we have a 'connection' to others."

Here's an example of a story from Melissa Bird-Vogel,

while she was a student in my Storytelling class:

I've been really into theater and film my whole life, acting in plays since 7th grade. Second Semester Junior Year of College, I was studying film at USC and Life was AWESOME. Then, one night, I was walking across the street and, unbeknownst to me, there was a car speeding along not paying attention to the upcoming crosswalk. I saw the car's headlights just before it struck me down, putting me into a coma. I (obviously) woke up, but with all the physical damage I was in a wheelchair. The doctors said it would take me about a year to walk again. The process was really difficult, and over time, I grew extremely discouraged.

Then I found out which play my school would be putting on in the fall: "Our Country's Good." The lead character of the play exemplified the redemptive power of theater and I was determined to learn how to walk in time to audition for the part. It was hard and I was barely off crutches when I returned to school, months before the doctors had thought possible… but I did it. I was walking, and I landed the part.

I then asked Melissa to tell her story again, using visuals

(still or moving images) in less than two minutes. It's an

effective short film, made more impressive by the fact that by

this point in the class, we had covered only storytelling structure

and the Action-Idea, and had deliberately not provided any

hands-on filmmaking training:

[http://vimeo.com/18776333]

Stories *are* universal. As a community-building activity,

they create bonds between participants, both in the act of story creation, and in story sharing. For communications professionals, be it marketer, journalist or PR practitioner trying to make sense of business models in turmoil, we are all faced with the fundamental challenge, "How do I engage people with my idea?" The answer is not "build a Facebook page." It begins with the initiation of a story strategy, one that is platform and channel agnostic. All those great social utilities, legacy media platforms and online channels can be deployed later as transaction enablers or accelerators. But engagement begins first and fundamentally with the story that we seek to tell.

As Scott Berkun, author of the bestselling *The Myths of Innovation* (O'Reilly Media, 2010) declared on my UWTV show *Media Space* in October 2010, "Technology can be a huge distraction to what is at the heart of all media: storytelling, and our irresistible need for narrative."

17. A Higher Level of Engagement

That same Media Space episode that concluded with
Berkun's commentary also featured the "godfather" of alternate
reality gaming (ARG), Elan Lee. Lee is so clearly at the
epicenter of the Storyteller Uprising, that it's worth watching
my entire conversation with him as he talks about his work
promoting a Stephen Spielberg film, a Nine Inch Nails album
and Microsoft's Xbox.

[http://youtu.be/yDIIGeW2Arw]

As for ARG -- Wikipedia's succinct definition works well:

An interactive narrative that uses the real world as a platform, often
involving multiple media and game elements, to tell a story that may
be affected by participants' ideas or actions.

So as Lee would say, traditional storytelling – books, TV,
movies – asks you to step out of your life for a while. ARG
calls on you to take a participative role in this form of
interactive story. But no matter how far Lee takes it, everything
he does begins with that foundational story. As an
entrepreneur, he doesn't mince words when it comes to the
communicative power of storytelling.

"If you want to manipulate someone, telling them do something is almost 100% ineffective," Lee told me. "Engage with them; make them feel a connection through characters, through emotion, through conflict."

"Manipulate" may sound strongly cynical, but as Carolyn Handler Miller argues in *Digital Storytelling* (Focal Press, 2008), we've been using this form of what she calls "narrative entertainment" for thousands of years. She says storytelling was "developed as a critical survival tool" in order to "convey important information about the environment, behavior of wildlife, and availability of food."

You could say that Elan Lee was also concerned about survival when he decided to put storytelling to effective use. A few years ago, he was growing frustrated with his friends who complained incessantly during the two terms of the Bush Administration, but took no action.

So he created a devious story platform, through a new line of t-shirts that contained hidden codes. As people discovered the placement of the codes, they could punch them in online and watch a short video. Strung together, the short films told the story of mysterious murder of a rock band's manager. Characters names included guitarist Jeff (as in "Thomas Jefferson"), Adam the bassist ("John Adams") and manager

Lynn ("Benjamin Franklin"). Slowly, it dawned upon the participants that they were receiving a backhanded education in the history of America's Founding Fathers.

It proved to be a successful campaign. Not only did the t-shirts get excellent product placement on an episode of *CSI New York*, but those who participated in Lee's t-shirt storytelling platform ended up forming voting parties and signed up for "Rock the Vote." For Elan Lee, and anyone else who employs storytelling to lead to a real world transaction, he had found a way to make a clear Return On Investment on his communication efforts through entertaining, interactive narrative.

18. Storytelling and Digital Media: 100 Stories

So yes, *The Myths of Innovation*'s Scott Berkun is right that the heart of all media begins with good storytelling. However, with the proliferation of inexpensive, easily accessible content creation and distribution technologies, we also have terrific new opportunities to engage others in imaginative new ways through story.

Ford Motor Company won the 2010 *Advertising Age* "Marketer of the Year" award for its groundbreaking Ford Fiesta campaign. The campaign's Action-Idea:

Ford wants to create buzz around its new subcompact car before it went on sale in the United States. But its target demographic of young drivers doesn't get Ford, and see it as a stodgy company that makes pickup trucks. So Ford recruits 100 "influencers" to take the Ford Fiesta on monthly missions for half a year, film their experiences and share their content and impressions with their friends online. Word of mouth builds, guaranteeing the car is a hit as it hits Ford's American showrooms.

This video explains how the Fiesta Movement worked: [http://youtu.be/QH-_WEHJfaE]

Ford surrendered "message" control to these passionate users so that they would tell their own stories in how they experienced the new car. By taking this unusual direction, it allowed Ford to connect to a larger community through technology and social media. There was also an authenticity to the narrative because it didn't originate from corporate headquarters, but from "real" people. Still, there is risk in authenticity, especially for a Fortune 100 company so accustomed to being in control. During his guest lecture in my Strategic Research class, Fiesta Brand Manager Sam De La Garza revealed that the Fiesta Agent campaign began before they started manufacturing the new car for the U.S. market. So the company had to source the 100 vehicles from their European factories. Only one of those cars had an automatic transmission. Very few of the Agents knew how drive with a manual gearbox.

Rather than kill what was certainly a public relations disaster in the making, Ford realized that there was no turning back (that's what you get for engaging social media influencers, once they're involved, you can't pull the plug without the whole world knowing). So the company acted entrepreneurially, and made a last minute decision to train all their agents how to drive stick over a long weekend at a racetrack in California. They didn't suffer through a single mishap throughout the entire campaign. And they met their sales target.

As Ford develops a more story-centric outreach strategy, it
made an unprecedented decision to fold its public relations and
marketing divisions into one – testimony to the rapidly
changing nature of communication, as paid media and earned
media blend into an overall strategy of story and engagement.
It's clear that the use of legacy media such as print and TV and
digital media are also morphing into one strategy.

It's a remarkable opportunity as the increasing availability
of these various communication channels allows us to reach out
to each other in different ways. The challenge remains
however: with this ability to transmit so much more, we are also
trying to manage how to receive so much more as well.
Choices abound.

Here's a simple formula: a high quality product (in other
words, a good story), tied to an entrepreneurial approach to
engagement, produced cost-effectively with a clear idea of what
constitutes success can reap strong ROI.

The British Broadcasting Corporation (BBC) did exactly
that in 2010. It challenged the British Museum to "justify the
museum in the digital age." The consensus was that the era of
"hang it and they will come" in the arts was long gone. Just
because a brand-name institution had curated what it estimated
was an important exhibit could no longer be assumed to be of

automatic appeal. People would now seek cultural experiences online rather than in a dusty old museum.

So the museum's director, Neil MacGregor, conceived *A History of the World in 100 Objects* – a weekly radio series for BBC Radio that year.

The series' Action-Idea was clear from the first episode:

The head of one of the world's leading museums, facing declining attendance, needs to remind people of the value proposition of his institution. He does so by telling, "the story through the things that humans have made" – one hundred of the museum's artifacts that he considers emblematic of this shared history. The stories of these objects bring that history to life, and inject renewed vibrancy to the museum's appeal.

"You're about to hear a sound of the past," MacGregor says at the outset of that first 14-minute episode, as he plays the sound of a dying star. The British Museum's director brings a delightful personal touch to his narrative, explaining that he selected Object 1/100 – the Mummy of Hornedjitef – because as a boy of eight, it was the first artifact he encountered when he visited the museum in 1954.

After cycling through the Maya maize god statue, a North American otter pipe, and a suffragette-defaced penny among 98 other objects, MacGregor comes full circle, returning to east Africa and a focus on the heavens with Object 100 – the portable solar panel. In doing so he tells the story of how solar panels are ultimately too expensive for rich countries given their huge energy demands but perfect for the world's poor with their more modest needs and abundance of sun. He stands atop the roof of the BBC to demonstrate the Chinese-made solar panel, and explains how the solar panel brings independence to so many people. In Kenya, a woman says it charges her mobile phone by day, connecting her to the global economy, and provides light at night. A series that began with a dying star ends with the hope that our solar system's very own star provides.

It was a multi-platform project that required no video – rather radio, podcast, participative website (users could submit stories about their own treasured historical objects) – and an instant hit, garnering four million listeners per episode, with 10 million podcast downloads worldwide. Engagement in the series was so great that the Museum said it could directly attribute an increase in year-over-year attendance to the success of *A History of the World in 100 Objects*. As MacGregor says, and so ably achieves through his remarkable storytelling strategy, "Telling history through things, is what museums are for."

19. Story as Common Denominator

This manifesto is not intended as a "how to guide." It's more "why you should" do as I and others have done; make the change and create your own uprising.

If you're looking to draw any sort of universal strategy from what I've outlined in these pages, this might help:

1. What's your Action-Idea?
2. Who would you like to engage?
3. What's your story plan (3 acts)?
4. Where would you like to distribute your story?
5. How will you engage your community?

My own professional transformation, the Arab spring, along with Ford and the British Museum's innovative campaigns are testimony to the monumental shift we are experiencing in media in the digital age. In the 20th century, separation between journalism and marketing was similar to the separation between church and state. One was an endeavor of inquiry in pursuit of the truth; the other was a promotional activity in pursuit of business success. Now, the two are synthesizing. Journalism is becoming more business-like as it strives for reinvention (and survival). Marketing is moving towards authenticity as it seeks a trusted connection with consumers who are no longer so easily funneled through a select number of media channels.

Ford faced a communication challenge in convincing young people that they still produced vehicles relevant to their interests. Rather than resort to a campaign of controlled message, this multinational corporation adopted an *entrepreneurial* strategy, relying on *innovative* technology-driven platforms to curate content from an influential *community*. Museum director Neil MacGregor faced a marketing challenge in his attempt to convince Britons of the ongoing value proposition of his institution. But rather than initiate yet another advertising campaign, he opted to create entertaining, trustful *stories* that celebrated the museum's formidable assets in a manner that reached a great number of people through a multiplicity of channels.

That's the "uprising" of our digital age — people seizing control of communication by building ongoing credible connection through story and digital technology. It's disruptive, it's real and it's happening right now. I highlighted those four words in the preceding paragraph – "entrepreneurship," "innovation," "community," "entertainment" – as I see them as the core elements that all communicators must now draw upon if they wish to engage with trust and persuasion in this noisy, chaotic digital age. Indeed, we call those elements the "Four Peaks" of the curricular focus of our Master of Communication in Digital Media program at the University of Washington. They imply the creation and curation of compelling stories in partnership with communities of interest, as we avail ourselves of connective technologies that by their very nature subvert our ability to entirely control the process. This brings both risk and opportunity, which we must manage on an ongoing basis if we are to achieve our stated Return on Investment in this communicative interaction. It all begins with getting someone's attention; it lives on through a sustained level of multi-platform engagement.

So, what's your story?

20. My Own Bitter Lesson: Detroit Uprising

If I'm going to advocate that effective 21st century communication consists of the dissemination of original content through an ongoing interaction with a community, then this manifesto must follow this same directive.

Since I wrote the first part, I've made it available as a free PDF download through the Storyteller Uprising blog, as well as an e-book, directing people to the link during my public appearances. As I continue with this project, I will modify these digital files, the print-on-demand edition, and hopefully, the enhanced multimedia e-book version. This is the same strategy that I employed with my *Independent America: The Two-Lane Search for Mom & Pop* film in 2005: the sharing of multiple iterations of the content even as I continue to develop it.

I did not take this approach with the sequel to *Mom & Pop* in 2008. Due to the success of the first film, we received an advance from our Canadian broadcaster to produce *Independent America: Rising from Ruins*. My premise was clear from the outset: how independent shopkeepers and restaurateurs in New Orleans were the first to return to rebuild the city after Hurricane Katrina in 2005, but faced an uneven playing field, thanks to preferential treatment local authorities were giving to big box stores.

Originally, I had set out to produce it in a similar manner to the first film. It would be a road trip that I would take with two of my students, documenting our quest to discover the "essence" of Independent New Orleans. Upon our arrival however, I quickly realized that this experience would be markedly distinct from the swashbuckling adventure of *Mom & Pop*. We were conducting powerful interviews with passionate characters. Ultimately, I would have them tell their own stories, and would not employ a third-person narration as we had with *Mom & Pop*. And with that, the pieces fell into place.

The feature-length documentary did well – in film festivals in New Orleans and Seattle, as well as in Canada on television. But it was not as successful as *Mom & Pop* when it came to word-of-mouth, DVD sales, and securing a US broadcaster. After all, *Mom & Pop* had aired in Australia, New Zealand, Japan, on two separate Canadian channels, and the Sundance Channel in America. It was featured in the first class section of Quantas Airlines, as well as on the homepages of Yahoo! News and Hulu. And it was reviewed positively in BusinessWeek, Fortune, USA Today and on ABC News.

So what happened to *Rising from Ruins*? I was distracted by the birth of our first child, as well as occupied with my new full-time job at the University of Washington; I wasn't as hungry to create buzz because we had the security of a broadcaster and finances from the outset; the independent film landscape had changed considerably with the economic downturn, with broadcasters having considerably more choices, given the explosion in the number of filmmakers taking advantage of the latest in inexpensive, new digital tools.

I've always considered *Rising from Ruins* to be a better film than *Mom & Pop* – substantively and production-wise. Though the Action-Idea was simple, it didn't have a clear protagonist driving that action, and most of the storytelling was after-the fact (the characters were relating stories two years previous). It was an impactful film, but it captured the intellect more than the imagination. You can watch it in its entirety for free, here:

[http://www.snagfilms.com/films/title/independent_america _rising_from_ruins/]

The question remains: were the story and the strategy around the distribution of that story sufficiently compelling to compete with the proliferation of content available at that time? *Mom & Pop* had been, but that was before the social media revolution that greatly facilitated the tactics we had used to produce and promote that film.

While filming in New Orleans, I learned from a local food security expert that America's urban farming epicenter was neither there, nor in Los Angeles, but surprisingly, in the heart of the rust-belt: Detroit. I knew that I had stumbled across the subject for my next film – I just needed the story.

It materialized two years later when I was invited to attend the Journalism That Matters organization's conference in Detroit, provocatively titled, "Create or Die." The organizers justified the event's location as the city's disintegrating economy could be seen as a metaphor for the transformation that journalism was also experiencing. The premise to the conference in many ways mirrors that of *Storyteller Uprising* – an opportunity for new forms of communication within new communities as the old models wither away:

For nearly 50 years, American journalism was financed by an historically unprecedented consumer-driven economy. This put pressure on editors, producers and reporters to focus on mainstream audiences attractive to advertisers. Cable television, and now the Internet, has made it economically feasible to profitably market to niche communities. For the first time, poor, ethnic and disadvantaged communities and under-represented constituencies of all economic strata are no longer too marginal to serve. Diverse constituencies must seize the opportunity to innovate with technology and services, legacy media must learn to include these new, niche audiences. Both creators and consumers die — figuratively, they lose influence or visibility — unless they understand the need to diversify.

I thought that the conference could provide me with the backdrop to access the energetic community activism occurring in a place that most Americans had given up for dead. So my friend and colleague Scott Macklin and I flew to Detroit with a half-developed notion to mash-up journalists looking for community-based solutions with residents finding self-sufficiency in their own efforts.

I had identified one particular neighborhood – Corktown – where we could do some reporting outside of the conference. I had done some light preparatory research, but no advance reporting. It may be a holdover from my overseas journalism days, but I enjoy the challenge of dropping into an unfamiliar place and searching for that inspiring story that happens to be hiding in plain sight. Still, I faced a huge narrative challenge: how could we connect a decidedly un-visual conference about journalism with urban farming?

We landed on our feet. I had identified a new restaurant, Le Petit Zinc, as our starting point. The chef/owner was from France; he grew his own produce. That was all I knew ahead of our arrival. Happily, the story began to tell itself from the moment that we hit Corktown. We ate lunch; we began to chat with the staff. It turned out that the chef's mother-in-law was the co-owner of the *Michigan Citizen* newspaper, housed in the very same building as the restaurant! The narrative connection between food and journalism was suddenly apparent. We began to meet more Corktown residents; some revealed how dissatisfied they were with how their stories were being told by outside media, as more interlopers descended upon Detroit to capture tales of woe and urban destitution in what locals had begun to call "ruins porn."

Perhaps it was time for their community to take control of their own narrative? We told them of our work as academics in digital media, and how we embraced this concept of the "storyteller uprising." Somehow, this alleviated their concerns of our being yet another couple of out-of-town "pornographers." With that, we began to make connections that led to a series of great interviews.

It was hard not to enjoy a brief moment of self-satisfaction as filmmakers who had stumbled across a developing story. At the same time as we were delving deeper into the community, the Journalism That Matters conference was in full swing.

One evening, we attended a talk by freelance reporter Karen Dybis, who had been contributing to Time Magazine's "Assignment Detroit" project (self-described as "One Year. One City. Endless opportunities"). Ahead of our arrival in the region, I had tried to contact one of the principal Detroit reporters from Time to see if we could visit the house the magazine had purchased to film their neighborhood bureau in action. I was dismayed when he refused, explaining that his team didn't want to open their office to the public. This was entirely contrary to the stated objectives of the project: to live within the community, be of that community, and tell real stories about its citizens.

Dybis' speech that evening was surprisingly blunt. She admitted that Time had screwed up from the outset of the project with its cover story, "The Tragedy of Detroit," along with its provocative imagery of desolation and abandonment. The Journalism That Matters participants began to talk excitedly among themselves. What if Time could donate the house at the end of the yearlong endeavor to a group of local Detroit storytellers, to continue the project in a more community-centric manner?

This possibility became a focal point as the conference moved into a pitch session to develop actionable projects that would explore new business models for journalism. Scott and I recognized that we had found ourselves in the middle of a nascent narrative that could serve as the central storyline for our film: an economically-devastated city that was learning how to feed itself through inspired community activism such as innovative urban farms, would also learn how to tell stories for itself – and not rely on outsiders to define who they were.

Despite being outsiders ourselves (!), this was the film that we set about to capture over the days that followed. But once we returned to Seattle, reality set in as my wife and I had another baby, with another academic year was imminent. So we didn't do what I always did at the completion of a shoot – which was screen the footage while it was still fresh in my mind.

It was strong material. Over the years, I had mastered the art of being a self-contained one-man studio, with camera, laptop and audio equipment. With both *Mom & Pop* and *Rising from Ruins*, I reviewed the footage every evening. I was still playing with new high-definition (HD) technology, so I wanted to be certain that everything was working. And given that my livelihood was at stake, I had a vested interest in ensuring that I was getting what I needed.

The Detroit project was different. We were shooting a short film as an exercise in storytelling that would hopefully be useful material for this book project. We had full-time jobs. No one had commissioned the film. Scott and I were seasoned filmmakers. I was now shooting on my tried and trusted Sony

EX-1 in uncompressed broadcast quality HD, easily editable on
my powerful Apple Macbook Pro laptop. Scott had just picked
up a Canon Rebel Single Lens Reflex (SLR) camera with
impressive HD video functionality. With this relatively small
device, he was capturing equally high resolution footage as I
was with my considerably more expensive setup, with the added
advantage that the remarkably sharp photographic lens of that
camera was bringing a heightened sense of professionalism to
our work with its shallow depth of field (the blurry background
that we have come to know and expect in Hollywood films and
high-end photography).

So we let the project sit. We engaged one of our students
to screen the material, make some notes, and based on our
guidance, put together a rough sequence that we could show in
our storytelling course. The class was unforgiving in its
criticism, employing much of what I've outlined in this book as
the basis for its evaluation of our work. The students rightfully
thought that we were trying to be too clever. They didn't quite
get the connection between urban farming and the conference.
They wanted us to establish Detroit's plight sooner than later,
and provide a sense of place. I was chastened, and
disheartened. Perhaps our film was not as good as we thought it

was. Take a look at this rough sequence and see what you think:

[http://vimeo.com/18678339]

Our fundamental problem was that we had not heeded the same lesson that we emphasize over and over again in class: we had never truly established a simple Action-Idea.

When the organizers of Journalism That Matters finally decided they could wait no longer for our final product and asked us for whatever we could give them so that they could promote their follow-up conference, I knew that I had to come up with something.

I watched the rough sequence a number of times. I realized that I had to establish the Action-Idea before I could proceed any further with the edit. This was one of my initial attempts:

Recognizing that the city of Detroit is on the ropes, its residents realize that they've got to help themselves. After Time Magazine paints a bleak picture of the town, a group of journalists attending a conference decide they need to take matters into their own hands. They conclude that they must make a bid to take over the magazine's city bureau.

I was getting closer to developing a tighter narrative, but it still felt uninspired and confused.

I thought about what Journalism That Matters was asking from us, and decided to consider it as "client" to help me craft the Action-Idea. This particular organization was looking for a

story solution to promote an event. So the first thing that I
needed to develop was an Action-Idea that actually
corresponded to that organization's objectives. Suddenly, I
began to make sense of what we had, at least within this
context. Here's what I ultimately printed out and taped to my
computer monitor as I began the next phase of the edit:

A group of journalists are looking to create new viable models for
their suffering profession. They decide to host a meeting in Detroit,
hoping to find inspiration in the community-based activism sprouting
up in this economically devastated city. While there, they hear of
Time Magazine's misguided "Assignment Detroit" reporting
experiment. The journalists realize that if Detroit is going to help
itself, it needs to take control of its own narrative, and rely less on
outsiders to tell their stories. This revelation encourages them to
petition Time to hand over their Detroit bureau to the community
when the assignment comes to an end.

By focusing on Journalism That Matters' needs, I was able
to put the participant journalists at the heart of the action, and
relegate the urban farming element to the film's backdrop. This
aligned the story with what the client wanted (telling the story
of the conference, encouraging others to register for their
upcoming event), and it maintained a simple storyline with an
obvious beginning, middle and end.

Here's the rough cut that I developed by holding tightly to
that Action-Idea taped to my computer monitor:

[http://vimeo.com/23069123]

At this point, I reengaged my colleague Scott in the project. He also had been feeling guilty about leaving it on the shelf for so long. As we talked it through, he admitted that although it had all the elements, the lack of a clear Action-Idea also made it difficult for him to get inspired to complete the film. Scott is also a visual ethnographer, and upholds the notion of "community-centric storytelling" – similar to the premise of our Detroit film where members of a community should be able to tell their own stories. However, Scott's concerns were alleviated by the tightly focused Action-Idea that I had crafted.

"We had done enough 'deep hanging-out' to tell the story behind the Action-Idea," he said to me. And with that, he set to work on the next cut of the film, adding music, effects, graphics, and still imagery through production software such as Final Cut Pro and After Effects. I had focused on footage mainly from my video camera, so with Scott's perspective, and with the footage he had shot on his Canon SLR, he was able to bring a more elaborate point-of-view into the film. But the Action-Idea continued to dictate his edit decisions.

"I used the arc to drive the images, music and effects I wanted to use," Scott said. "How we saw Detroit through the car window. How we were moving fast, shooting up to eight interviews each day. People were moving; the music had to embody that."

We're both strong proponents that story needs to drive the choices that we make in the field, and in the edit suite. By tying the film directly to the context of the conference, our task was greatly simplified. Whose interests are being served? Who is the content for? This focus helped us to determine scope, voice, and even the length of the film. This was not going to be a theatrical release, Journalism That Matters needed it quickly to promote its upcoming event, and so the web version would suffice. In that case, the general rule of thumb was to keep online content to less than five minutes, given limited attention spans. Our final cut was eight minutes, and we left it at that because we believed that's what it took to tell the story properly. We also hoped that anyone who was interested in the mission of Journalism That Matters would consider that amount of time a worthwhile investment. By no means was this going to be a film festival award-winning short. But with its focused narrative, anyone who was thinking hard about the future of journalism, would not find this film's duration daunting, and would probably watch it to the end.

Here's the final cut of *Detroit Uprising*:
[http://vimeo.com/]

21. Practical Matters: The Tools You Need

Effects aside, *Detroit Uprising* is a fairly straightforward short film. These days, basic film editing is no more complicated than creating a graphics-heavy word processing document. It's just a matter of practice. What matters most is crafting an appropriate story, then choosing the appropriate tools to put that story together. Software, computers, cameras have all become considerably more accessible over the last two decades. The HD technology that I used to shoot that particular film cost less than $10,000. Ten years ago, it would have set me back six figures, and I would have needed to hire a professional post-production company to edit the tapes.

Although we stress in our digital media graduate program that the best camera is the one that you have on hand, I do maintain a list of bare minimum equipment if you want to produce your own multimedia stories:

- A camera (low end around $200 that shoots HD video, ideally has an external microphone jack; if you have more money consider a digital SLR still camera that shoots video or a higher-end HD video camera ($800-$3500).

- A good quality tripod ($80 for a small camera, up to $500 for a medium-sized camera.

- An external microphone ($80 for a small, consumer-grade camera, up to $1,000 for a more professional "shotgun" microphone. You may also want to consider a wireless lapel mike set).

- I believe fundamentally in the importance of good sound – it matters more than video. If your camera does not have an external mike input, then I would suggest purchasing a stand-alone digital audio recorder for around $300. You can record your audio separately from your video and then marry the two in the edit suite later (which is traditionally how filmmakers work).

- A basic lighting kit. Most professionals carry at least three lights; I'm more run-and-gun, and not particularly good at setting up lights, so I stick to one, high quality light.

- A laptop with a good sized hard drive and robust video card for HD editing. If this is your only computer, get at least a 15" high-resolution screen.

- A non-linear editing system. I like Sony Vegas, Adobe Premiere, Avid, or Final Cut Pro. They range in price and complexity from $100 to $2,500.

That's really all you need to get started to produce high quality content for the web, or even occasionally for television. If you'd like to learn more about basic shooting and lighting, I highly recommend Barry Braverman's *Video Shooter: Storytelling with HD Cameras* (Taylor & Francis, 2009).

Should your budget be further constrained or if you're looking to have something more portable on hand (as I always do, subscribing to the survivalist's notion of always being "loaded for bear" – in a state of perpetual readiness to get that great story when it happens), you may want to consider the following basics:

- A point-and-shoot camera with HD video functionality, or a smartphone with a high quality lens.

- A small tabletop tripod.

- An ultraportable notebook computer or tablet with basic editing software (iMovie, Premiere Elements or Sony Vegas).

Music is readily available through a variety of royalty-free websites, or you can create your own thanks to a number of simple soundtrack creation programs that employ music loops and sound effects. You want to ensure that you do not include copyright-protected material in your content. When it comes to legalities such as these, I would go as far as to get written permission from anyone who appears in your multimedia content, and from property owners if you happen to be producing your content in private premises.

Clearly, it's easy to get hung up on the barriers to your first stories – be they technological, legal or skills-related. But never forget that the uprising can begin with the tiniest of sparks – such as a powerful scene captured on a shaky cellphone camera. In the end, the feelings that you convey and inspire through your story are what will move people to action. The digital tools merely enable the production and promulgation of that catalyzing narrative.

22. Make The Change

Our world is changing. It's not incremental change. It's a wholesale transformation, wrought by technology and globalization. Industries are dying; others are being born. Business models are disappearing; new ones are crystallizing. Once-powerful countries are in decline; once-feeble ones are emerging.

Revolution is the most extreme form of change; it's a transformation that doesn't happen without stories. As Eric Selbin argues in *Revolution, Rebellion, Resistance: The Power of Story* (Zed Books, 2010), "[S]tories allow us to imagine the transformation of our lives and the world…to tell, to share news, information and much more; to guide, to warn, to inspire, to make real and possible that which may well be unreal and impossible." They remind us that wholesale change has happened in the past, and will happen again. This simple act of sharing information – storytelling – also reminds us that we're not alone in our fears and aspirations.

Those stories have precipitated change for thousands of years as we inspire and discover each other. Online social networks have quickened the pace of that change. As we create stories, not only can we share them broadly with people we have never met, those same people can be inspired to interact with others, often in real time. That inspiration can be so deep, that they might even choose to create their own stories, expanding the creative cycle well beyond the intent (and control) of the original storyteller.

The Stranger columnist Dan Savage merely wanted to provide a beacon of hope to lesbian, gay, bisexual and transgender (LGBT) teens when he created his own video, *It Gets Better*. The Seattle journalist had been horrified when Billy Lucas, a bullied 15 year-old in Indiana, took his own life. Savage wanted to inspire others facing similar torment that they could endure and emerge as fully-formed members of society, just as he had. "There really is a place for us, there really is a place for you," Savage said on the video. "Life gets better, and the bigots don't win."

[http://youtu.be/7IcVyvg2Qlo]

Within weeks, regular citizens, movie stars, musicians, mayors, and heads of state – including the President of the United States -- were posting their own videos of support and sharing them on the YouTube channel. The campaign has produced over 20,000 videos with 50 million views and counting. It is said to have saved lives and has led to substantive policy change. *It Gets Better* exemplifies the ability of anyone to effect seismic social change at a near instantaneous pace -- through the equalizing access of readily available digital platforms.

In this way, individuals can create change that was once primarily enabled and filtered by institutional media channels. It's an accomplishment that we at the Master of Communication in Digital Media program recognize as representative of a new set of best practices in effecting behavioral change through persuasive media. That's why we selected Savage and his husband Terry Miller as recipients of the MCDM's "Make The Change" Award in 2011. In his acceptance video, Savage observed how he knew that he had to connect directly to teens while they were still in school, but he also acknowledged that those schools' administrations would never invite him.

"It occurred to me in a flash that in the YouTube era, I was waiting for permission that I no longer needed," Savage said. "That I had the tools at my disposal to sit down and share my story to illuminate that path."

Savage's acceptance speech for the "Make The Change" Award bears watching to better understand how he achieved so much with so few resources, and without institutional support:

[http://vimeo.com/25045566]

Dan Savage created compelling content (the story), and injected it into the media ecosystem. Its powerful narrative inspired others to comment, share and respond to the story. Savage recognized that a community was forming around his initial video, and developed the *It Gets Better* campaign. That community began to create its own story assets, feeding acts of engagement that the original storyteller could have hardly anticipated (nor had the resources to do himself). In this way, a sustainable story cycle was created.

23. The Art of Strategic Storytelling

The same best practices that now produce such profound social change, can also serve an organization's outreach objectives as well. Indeed, the global public relations firm Weber Shandwick (to which I have served as counsel) has put this form of communication and engagement at the center of its "Art of Storytelling" strategy for its clients.

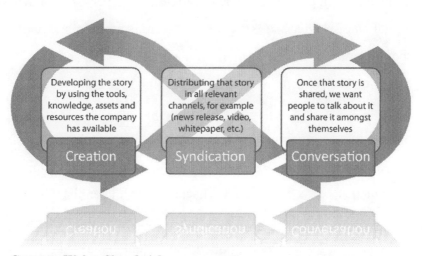

Courtesy Weber Shandwick

The marketing equivalent to the success and reach of *It Gets Better* is Old Spice's *The Man Your Man Could Smell Like*. As of writing this chapter (fall 2011), the Old Spice campaign is the most successful viral video in the young history of the Web.

[http://youtu.be/owGykVbfgUE]

It was developed by a team of young professionals at Wieden+Kennedy, a Portland, Oregon-based advertising agency.   What follows is a deconstruction of their incredible success.

I must stress at the outset however, that as Weber Shandwick has signposted through its own strategy, storytelling is an "art."   All of us who hope to influence and persuade in the digital maelstrom are looking for the "secret sauce" in how we should communicate.   But this is not a process; it's a creative endeavor, and we can no more assure a viral video as we can manufacture another musical sensation like The Beatles. Storytelling is iterative.   As I have experienced far too often myself as a creator, it requires risk, courage, experimentation and practice.   This bears further discussion in a later chapter.

The Wieden+Kennedy team had owned the Old Spice body wash account for five years, which I saw them explain at a standing-room only session of the March 2011 South by Southwest Interactive Conference in Austin, Texas.   They experimented considerably, hoping to gain ground against a surging competitor: Unilever's Axe product.

Their client, Proctor & Gamble, gave them two days to develop a new concept, leaving them "not a lot of time to overthink." Their research had revealed that although men used Old Spice body wash, it was usually their female partners who purchased the product. That set the creative process in motion.

The team decided to employ an integrated approach to introducing their content into the media ecosystem, with a combination of a clever TV ad launched on Super Bowl weekend, followed by digital distribution. There was no guarantee that anyone would like what they had created – a strangely humorous exhortation from a former professional football player wearing only a towel – but what happened next could have hardly been anticipated. Americans flocked to the ad, they shared it, they commented on it, and they spoofed it (with a notable Sesame Street parody). Oprah Winfrey declared her love for it; Ellen DeGeneres interviewed Isaiah Mustafa the actor who played the "Old Spice Man" on her show.

And yet, at this point, *The Man Your Man Could Smell Like* was still nothing more than a really successful advertisement, with some staying power thanks to social media. It was what Wieden+Kennedy did five months later with the *Old Spice Responses* strategy that truly set the web afire, with 6 million YouTube channel views within a 24-hour period.

[http://www.youtube.com/playlist?list=PL484F058C3EAF
7FA6]

With a scant (by advertising standards) $200,000 budget,
they set up a makeshift film studio in their Portland office.
They employed a social media team to analyze online
conversations in real-time, and the Old Spice Man began to
respond directly to comments and requests that had been left on
YouTube, Facebook and Twitter. In two days, they created 186
videos that played exclusively on Old Spice's YouTube
channel. Their responses focused on influencers, along with a
few celebrities such as actor Ashton Kutcher and his wife, Demi
Moore.

[http://youtu.be/GPlg9ez4L1w]

Thanks to their social media monitoring, they identified
individuals who carried considerable weight within their own
online communities such as Kevin Rose, the founder of Digg,
and (bravely) the controversial Internet collective
"Anonymous." It was a highly entrepreneurial, interactive
engagement strategy that reaped considerable dividends, in both
brand awareness (the Old Spice YouTube channel has over 200
million views as of this writing) and in sales (which increased
110% at the height of the campaign).

24. The Storytelling Brief

Restating that the scale of Old Spice's success can't be readily achieved, we can still draw out a set of steps from that campaign for the strategic storyteller to follow. I've outlined those steps in bold, with how Wieden+Kennedy might have followed them with *The Man Your Man Could Smell Like* in italics. It's a useful template for anyone interested in developing a story engagement strategy for his or her organization.

(a) What outcome do you seek (ideally based on recent, specific insights that you might have around your initiative or product)? Such as behavior change, product launch, increase in sales, brand awareness, donation.

Revitalization of Old Spice as a brand for men, specifically Body Wash purchases by their female partners.

(b) What kind of successful engagement needs to occur? Such as online comments, increase in word of mouth, social media affirmation.

Need to get online users (primarily women) talking about Old Spice, sharing story assets, having conversation as couples about body wash.

(c) What story do you want to tell?

Considering your organization's overall narrative, develop a short Action-Idea.

An absurdly attractive man asks women if they'd like their partners to look like him. He confesses that this isn't possible. But if they can smell like him by using Old Spice Body Wash, the other desires these women crave could be fulfilled.

(d) What are your story's primary elements?

In other words, what might create a relevant, relatable connection, set the scene, provide some narrative tension, as well as a resolution?

A half-naked man with a toned body pleads that women look at him; he tempts them with alluring objects and exotic settings that flash by in a humorous way; then offers up Old Spice Body Wash as a solution with a final punch line.

(e) What is your story format and vehicle?
Such as a video, podcast, text, game, press release, blog, slideshow, whitepaper or an online series.

A series of short commercial videos, destined for web and TV.

(f) How will you syndicate your story into the media ecosystem?
Consider your organization's channels, social channels and legacy media channels.

Online distribution Super Bowl weekend (when couples are together), followed by TV broadcast the day after the Super Bowl when people are searching online for event-related commercials.

(g) What conversations and interactions can you anticipate from this syndication?
Consider how you can engage any influencers involved in those conversations and interactions.

Comments on YouTube, blogs, Facebook, Twitter, other social platforms. Sharing via those networks and e-mail.   Identify influencers' feedback (highly respected commenters, high Klout scores, celebrities, well known figures within specific communities).

(h) What further story assets can you develop from those conversations and interactions (sometimes in collaboration with your influencers) that will help propagate and sustain your story ecosystem?

Choose a number (186) of commenters (primarily influencers) and respond directly to them with time-sensitive online videos using the same actor and action-idea over a weekend

25. Stories Change Organizations

Old Spice, *It Gets Better*, *A History of the World in 100 Objects*, the Arab Spring and the Ford Fiesta campaign are all examples of successful storytelling undertakings. They produced compelling content, grabbed the attention of a large number of online users, and often employed legacy media such as TV or radio, or were further amplified by them once achieving a certain level of popularity.

The communities of interest that form around these stories can do so nearly instantaneously, and dissipate just as quickly as they move on to the next shiny bright object. The most sustainable ones are those that aren't entirely dependent upon a single source of original content. In other words, their host organizations may need to see their story strategy as an ongoing, standalone media channel fed by a team of contributors (be they paid professionals akin to journalists for a multimedia magazine or volunteer members of the community who are passionate enough to push new content).

Although some best practices are beginning to emerge as storytelling takes hold as an effective communications strategy, it will never be an easy "check the boxes" endeavor. Clay Shirky observed in *Here Comes Everybody*, that when you change how society communicates, you change society. The same applies to organizations. Any entity that seeks to integrate an authentic, trusted channel of communication, harvesting stories internally, producing them externally must be prepared for a degree of structural transformation.

I've discovered this as I begin to work with large companies that seek to create "internal newsrooms" to curate and disseminate stories. In this way, these professional communicators hope to connect more authentically and persuasively to their various communities of interest. Does storytelling reside within the Marketing Department? Public Relations? How about Customer Service? This is perhaps one reason why Ford Motor Company opted to merge its marketing and public relations into one department in 2010, in recognition of the new communications reality.

Stories can't be easily manufactured by a bureaucratic system. To be effective, they must have meaning. Stories must be found, grown, and nurtured. If you have the resources of a large organization, you can hire an agency to do much of the heavy lifting for you. But even then, you'll still need to deputize as many of your own constituents to keep an eye on the latest developments and interactions with customers, clients and partner organizations. Those interactions ultimately become new story assets and can lead to a more sustainable story channel. It may not necessarily require substantial funding, but it could precipitate a fundamental change in point of view: that every employee or volunteer is a potential storyteller.

26. Dark Nights of the Soul (and Helping Hands)

It's a heavy charge, to acknowledge that we all have the ability to act as storytellers. As inherent as story may be to all of us, storytelling itself is not an action easily initiated as the flicking of a switch.

Rather, it's a metaphoric hard road to follow: one that's poorly signposted and often unpaved, fraught with hairpin curves that can scarcely afford the comfort of emergency shoulders. That's the inescapable truth of really good storytelling: it's a creative act with skills that can only be developed by doing – and on a regular basis.

I've taught storytelling through a ten-week class, and even then, I knew my students were just getting started. The creation of something new is not *meant* to be easy. When I wish to impress this upon anyone who wishes to become a more public storyteller, I like to refer to one of my own favorite storytellers, author and journalist George Orwell. The author of classics such as *1984* and *Animal Farm* concluded his famous 1946 essay *Why I Write*, with some fairly daunting words:

Writing a book is a horrible, exhausting struggle, like a long bout of some painful illness. One would never undertake such a thing if one were not driven on by some demon whom one can neither resist nor understand. For all one knows that demon is simply the same instinct that makes a baby squall for attention. And yet it is also true that one can write nothing readable unless one constantly struggles to efface one's own personality. Good prose is like a windowpane. I cannot say with certainty which of my motives are the strongest, but I know which of them deserve to be followed.

There is a strong intangible catalyst to want to create a story. At first, it's a heady thing to believe that we can rise above the mundane and bring a new, compelling idea into the world. The beginning is often easy. It's that indefinable, muddle of the middle that causes such difficulty, when confidence wears thin and we're no longer sure of the creative direction that we've chosen.

That's exactly what happened to my wife and me as we hit Texas while filming *Independent America*. We suddenly realized that we were armed with but the thread of an idea – this nascent insurgency against corporate chain retail. We were spending the last of our savings on a mad dash across the country. Would anyone really want to pay attention to what we were doing? To what we had to say? As we checked into the Austin Motel, I was ready to call it quits. With three quarters of our trip still ahead of us, wouldn't it be better if we ran back to the security of home, and maybe a full-time job? This is what artists call the "dark night of the soul" when all seems lost, and

it seems better to turn back than to forge ahead. It's a spiritual
moment, despite its bleakness. As a creator, you're best to
accept its inevitable occurrence and just wait to see what
happens next in that artistic purgatory.

In our case, just as we were set to retreat in shame, we
received a call from Wal-Mart's corporate communications
office. They had read our blog. They had seen the video clips
we had posted online. They would do an on-camera interview
with us if we could make it up to Bentonville, Arkansas.

It was as if the heavens had opened, as unforeseen pairs of
helping hands emerged. While biding our time in Austin before
we turned north for the Wal-Mart interview, I re-connected with
a woman I had interviewed years before in Israel when Saddam
Hussein threatened Scud missile attacks against the Jewish
state. Chris DeWitt was so enthralled with our film's premise
that she would end up serving as our publicist and associate
producer, helping us build incredible momentum with
community newspapers and local public radio stations as we
continued on our trek. And a young Kosovar for whom I had
helped secure Canadian refugee status a few years back when I
was covering the Balkan conflict for NBC, ended up creating
most of the film's soundtrack (I will admit that one reason I was

originally drawn to Hyshi Kantarxhiu was that he was a huge fan of guitar god Joe Satriani).

Nearly a year later, with our nascent independent media venture well underway, Heather and I were driving down a dirt track in Botswana's Kalahari Desert. We had been hired by the US government to shoot a series of stories about economic development in southern Africa. As we had been in Texas, we were exhausted, and questioning our decision to become entrepreneurs. The farmer we had been seeking to profile was speeding ahead in his four-wheel drive, even as I continued to spin around, unable to keep up with him. I just couldn't get any traction in the loose dirt. I put it down to my substandard vehicle and its city tires. I threw up my hands in exasperation, and refused to drive an inch further.

The farmer drove back to meet up with us, and asked why we couldn't keep up. I explained the problem to him in a frustrated tone. He may have also spotted that my knuckles were white, from grasping the steering wheel so tightly.

"You're doing it wrong," he said. "Take your hands off the wheel. Let the road guide you."

It seemed improbable, but I really didn't have any other choice. I hit the gas, and did exactly that. The road's deep parallel grooves held us tight like a locomotive on a train track.

And I stopped steering. It made all the difference. We sped quickly and securely towards our destination.

The larger lesson was clear. We can try and plan our direction to the smallest possible detail before setting out on the journey – or creating a story. But in this digital age, when communication is fluid, and so many people are experimenting, often the best thing to do is to simply get in the car, take your hands off the wheel, keep your eyes on the road, and hit the gas. As we discovered, the universe has unusual ways of assisting those who decide to engage in creative pursuits.

We did our best to research and plan the best foreseeable outcome for *Independent America* for nearly a year. But after failing to convince any large media institution of the idea's worth, we finally listened to our friends and family who had been prodding us on to just get out there and do it. They gave us money, ideas and crucial moral support. Just as Dan Savage had learned with *It Gets Better*, we really didn't have to wait for institutional approval. The idea was good, we believed in it passionately, and we had the tools and time at our disposal. We would soon discover that the road – and the community that would inspire us—would take us the rest of the way.

27. Inconspicuous, Ubiquitous, Sociable

I watched the live feed, amazed. It looked like a "real" newscast, the kind you see on a 24-hour cable channel when news is "breaking."

There was the shaky, raw footage putting us in the heart of the action, a ticker at the bottom of the screen laying out the latest developments leading up to this occurrence.

But there was no self-assured anchor bantering with the reporter at the scene, no commercial break, and no instantly recognizable logo in the corner of the screen. Nor was there a satellite truck, a news chopper, a camera crew, or anyone seemingly in charge.

It had been some random Twitter update that drew me to the site. The police were raiding the Occupy Wall Street protest camp at Zuccotti Park in lower Manhattan. The counter in the bottom right hand corner of the screen read 14,000 viewers when I joined in. Twenty minutes later, there were over 20,000. Several of these participants were commenting on the video they were collectively witnessing via a discussion feed on the right side of the screen. Whoever was transmitting the video footage was also providing helpful scrolling updates below the live images: "Police are throwing everything;" "Park surrounded;" "Possible LRAD on site."

I wondered how long the New York Police Department would tolerate the coverage, especially as I had just quickly checked in on the New York Times website and read that journalists had been shut out of the area. Would some official find a way to shut down whatever tenuous Internet connection was keeping the flow of live images flowing to screens like mine?

Later, I would discover that the media creation and distribution infrastructure behind the Occupy movement was the polar opposite to what I had encountered in 1994 when I started at NBC News. And it was much more user-friendly (and inexpensive) than the nascent "backpack journalist" technology that I had helped pioneer during the second Gulf war. Indeed, as *Wired* magazine reported in November 2011, GlobalRevolution.TV began with a single roving camcorder, a laptop and a 4G wireless card on the first day of the Occupy Wall Street protests, using the Livestream platform to share the real-time visuals with anyone who navigated to http://www.livestream.com/occupynyc. Two months later, they would have a few more mobile hotspots at their disposal, a set of Dell laptops purchased for $400 on eBay, all housed in a "narrow room on the second floor of a rundown building, filled with cobbled-together gear and a hint of body odor."

And that was just one of the media operations supporting this vastly decentralized movement. Former skateboard videographer Tim Pool became famous for capturing much of the raid on his Android-based Samsung Galaxy S2 mobile phone, and transmitting through Ustream.com via his carrier's 3G connection. During the raid of November 17th, 2011, he would get 737,000 unique viewers; Pool's material would be rebroadcast by Al Jazeera English, and picked up by other outlets, according to *Fast Company* magazine.

This event – and the way it was covered – points to the future of storytelling and the technology that supports it. Let's look first at what this means for humans and how we tell stories.

New York University's Jay Rosen is famous for having coined the term, "the people formerly known as the audience" on his *PressThink* blog in 2006. "The people formerly known as the audience wish to inform media people of our existence," he wrote, "and of a shift in power that goes with the platform shift you've all heard about."

Obviously, Rosen was thrilled by Tim Pool's "citizen journalism" during the Occupy raids. He included a reader's letter in his post about Pool, which observed that the young videographer was acting as the "eyes and ears" for his viewers; when they asked him to do something, he would act almost instantly, from moving his camera, to conducting an interview at their behest. "But it goes both ways" Chris Fornof wrote to Rosen:

When his camera battery goes low, people swarm into action. Purchasing batteries, locating someone on the ground to deliver, and coordinating delivery. He's got a dozen batteries, pack and chargers just donated to him so he can keep recording. He mentions he's getting hungry and somehow people make sure he's fed with a constant stream of random strangers exactly what he needs when he needs it. This also extends to a few thousand people that will devour twitter and live news feeds to give him active intel so he can stay safe.

The goodwill he's engendering is ridiculous [italics mine]. Beyond the participation, there's relationships happening here. I have never seen this kind of support for a journalist before. He logs off for the night and hundreds of people stream in their 'THANK YOU!'s and undying gratitude."

[http://pressthink.org/2011/11/occupy-pressthink-tim-pool/]

It's this symbiotic relationship between storyteller and "the people formerly known as the audience" that speaks to the power of producing content through our own channels. It's trust, it's accountability, it's often real-time and it's highly responsive. And the ideas (from Occupy to Tea Party, Arab Spring to It Gets Better) carried by these highly accessible, highly democratized stories often propelled by seemingly leaderless movements are shaking the hierarchical, infrastructure-heavy systems we had become so inured to over the last six decades. This can only mean that we're in for more change and uprisings, as the technology that transports these narratives becomes even more pervasive, portable, and cheap.

Wired's GlobalRevolution.TV profile revealed Occupy volunteer Lorenzo Serna as the producer of that Livestream feed I had watched of the police raid. Serna's thoughts of the future hint at where we may be headed:

"Lorenzo Serna fantasizes about a multimedia outfit, consisting of a wearable camera and a heads-up display, so he can see his own video feed, watch the chat stream coming from viewers around the world, and respond in real time."

[http://www.wired.com/threatlevel/2011/11/inside-ows-media-hq/]

This is no longer the stuff of science fiction. Serna dreams of innovations that will feed a highly interactive form of storytelling in the coming years. These devices will be readily available to consumers – inconspicuous, ubiquitous and highly sociable. So here's my educated guess at what's on the immediate horizon.

(1) Inconspicuous devices

Those Spartan (a couple of USB ports at most, no optical drive) ultrabooks, exemplified by the Macbook Air, point the way to near-pocketable powerful computing. But these thin and light laptops will be reserved for activities that require more processor-intensive activities (such as elaborate video editing). It's the smartphone that will act as our personal computing hub, connected to other devices attached to our body: from wristwatches that show us the latest text message, to eyeglasses that "augment" our reality with graphical overlays and information (say as we tour an historical site), even as they capture video, to sensors in our clothing that detect our movement, measure our calories, distance and body heat. We will produce and consume real-time data that will drastically alter our awareness and actions, even as we untether ourselves from our desks. After all, we'll no longer need keyboards, mice, or remote controls, thanks to voice navigation and motion detection.

(2) Ubiquitous networking

Wireless networks at home and in the office, along with cellular antennae and mobile hot spots were just the first steps to keeping us in a perpetual state of connection, irrespective of our location. But these technologies are either limited in distance or by bandwidth. Two developments – one certain, the other still in experimental stages – will erode these boundaries.

The next frontier for network accessibility? The automotive industry. Manufacturers such as Ford and Mercedes are set to install Wi-Fi hot spots in their vehicles. Ostensibly, it begins as a safety feature: cars can now communicate with each other when they come into range, warning them off should they get too close for comfort. But once you establish a connection, there's so much more that you can do with it. Tether your devices, dump your local radio station/stream your favorite online music service, uninstall those rear passenger DVD players/stream from your preferred video entertainment provider to your tablet, put aside that Bluetooth audio connection/stream your conversation (and your view) through Skype. Suddenly movements such as Occupy might have the equivalent of a TV satellite truck in a compact car that an activist say, borrows from her parents. And our increasingly bird's-eye view of our world will now extend to the reach and mobility of the visuals that we can capture through our automobile.

But where are we going to get the bandwidth for all of these new ways to consume data? We're all too well aware of

the congestion (and commensurate bandwidth caps) we're
experiencing on our broadband and cellular networks.

How about in the "white space?" As television has made
the transition to a much more efficient digital frequency, it's
said to no longer need a certain part of the spectrum that in
America, the Federal Communications Commission (FCC) had
reserved for as "white space" to reduce potential signal
interference. Suddenly we may have unfettered access to a
form of "Wi-Fi on steroids" with a range of up to six miles
according to *Connected World Magazine* in December 2011:

All a customer or business needs to do to use TV white spaces is plug
in a TV white space base station, connect it to the Internet, then
authenticate whatever TV white space devices they want to use with
the base station, and they're on the air. TV white spaces' large
coverage areas allow colleges, businesses, communities, and farmers
to inexpensively set up fast local data networks that cover their entire
campus or ranch. Microsoft installed a "white fi" network at its
Redmond, Wash., headquarters in late 2010, covering all 500 acres of
the campus with only two TV white space base stations. It would take
hundreds of Wi-Fi routers to cover the same area. Local businesses
can track valuable things and people within a six-mile radius, using a
network that is simple and doesn't require contracting with a mobile
operator or monthly fees.

A few caveats about white space: it exists in varying
degrees depending on a city's available spectrum. And true to
form, the U.S. Congress is looking to raise money off of the
auction of some of this spectrum (even as the FCC had already

stated that it would be made available for unlicensed use). Still, access to this kind of connectivity would facilitate the distribution of expansive amounts of content (especially live, high definition video), potentially disrupting the business models of cellular and cable providers, providing new opportunity for widespread distribution of stories.

(3) Sociability around content

At the height of TiVo's popularity in North America, many of us were proclaiming the death of television. Time shifting through digital video recorders such as TiVo meant that viewers could skip over commercials and watch programs whenever they wanted. So why would advertisers want to pay such a heavy premium to broadcasters if no one was watching?

But we forgot one thing. Television remains our electronic water cooler. People commune around the "happening" of a TV program. Our love affair with television content is still a lingua franca for popular culture, even as the Internet fragments everything else. And suddenly, there's a new reason to watch TV in real time – so that we can interact with others in that same real time. It's an attractive proposition for anyone who uses media as connective tissue because it presents the possibility of creating an *immersive* experience (a deep engagement with the ideas that underlie the content).

An early indication of this was Barack Obama's Presidential Inauguration in January 2009. CNN partnered with Facebook to stream the live event and facilitate conversations. According to Mashable.com, 4,000 people a minute were commenting on the Facebook CNN feed, with a total of 600,000 status updates. Suddenly, we have the marriage between traditionally passive medium of television and the sometimes hyperactive buzz of social media, enabled through the so-called "second screen" of computers, mobile devices and tablets. Even as we're watching TV, we have an eye fixed on another screen.

As we saw with the Occupy movement, those social interactions can have a profound impact on the live event itself (camera angles, interviews), which would emphasize the renewed interactivity between storyteller and community. We've been so used to qualifying those who watch TV as "audience" that it may take some courage to acknowledge that when audience members begin to truly engage with each other and the content that has given them common cause, they actually transform into a "community," with common interests, shared values, mutually-agreed upon rules and a strong degree of trust.

My students led me to this important progression of audience to community after I had assigned them to produce a blog and build "community" around it (which happens to be the premise of this book). But as several of them pointed out, "community" isn't readily created. It takes time, work, and a degree of self-identification with a common cause. So, yes, I must admit that once you establish your narrative Action Idea, it's helpful to then ask, "who is your audience?" (a broader, more passive and established entity). Later you can determine whether the stories that you tell might inspire a deeper form of audience loyalty leading to the social cohesion of community. Once you have catalyzed that kind of commitment, then convincing your followers to engage in some form of transformation – be it behavioral change or a wholesale uprising – becomes that more probable.

So what could this mean for the Lorenzo Sernas of the near future? They'll be even more inconspicuous with cameras integrated into their eyeglasses or somewhere in their clothing, recording the footage remotely on a smartphone hidden away comfortably in their pocket. From the ground, they'll control an inexpensive drone helicopter overhead, capturing 3D aerials of the scene (because 3D by then will have proven itself to be an essential element of that immersive "you are there" experience). A production team will be stationed in a nearby car, taking in the various feeds thanks to the portable white space network they've created through an in-vehicle router, uploading them to an online streaming site. Passionate members of the viewing community will interact with the content and the production teams through traditional text conversations, as well as visual Google+-like "hangouts," manipulated by voice and physical gestures. A third party organization will capture these multiple streams and multiplicity of interactions, repackaging them and broadcasting them to an even larger audience on more mainstream social media and television channels. In the aggregate, this powerful story will have the production values of a Hollywood blockbuster, the impactful intimacy of a weekly gathering in a small town church, and the social consequence of history being made, discussed, recorded and transmitted – all in real time. This is no "brave new world," it is a very real media-driven uprising – coming soon to a street corner, marketplace and institution near you.

28. A Storyteller's Seven Hard Truths to Manipulation in a Networked World

I've written this book and published it in stages over the last two years. This is the final section, which intended as a standalone piece with first-time bibliographical that advances and concludes Storyteller Uprising.

The important thing about songs is that they're just like stories – they don't mean a damn unless there's people listening to them. – *Anansi Boys*, Neil Gaiman

The proliferation of online networks and the popularization of the social media that fill those networks have inspired a surge of interest in storytelling. Both individuals and organizations recognize that while we have this newfound ability to connect to others without the direct, editorial intervention of media institutions, we still need to find a compelling, friction-free way to capture people's attention and engage them. Stories provide a simple solution as they embody an activity that has been so engrained in us as human beings. As renowned mythologist Joseph Campbell so aptly observed throughout his life's work (particularly in *The Hero with a Thousand Faces*), stories help us make sense of our own lives, even as we move through our own three-act play, from childhood, to maturity and ultimately to our decline. So we're more likely to pay attention to them when we can make that narrative connection. Similarly, in a beautiful, short documentary film, *Ken Burns: On Story* (Tom Mason, Sarah Klein directors, Redglass Pictures, 2012) the famed documentarian of the American civil war, baseball and national parks declares, "We have to keep the wolf from the door. We tell stories to continue ourselves. We all think an exception is going to be made in our case and we're going to live forever. Being a human, is actually arriving at the understanding that that's not going to be. Story is there to just remind us that it's just okay."

[http://vimeo.com/40972394]

In *Storyteller Uprising: Trust and Persuasion in the Digital Age,* I make the case for storytelling's deep relevance in our 21st century communication ecosystem, through my own work as a filmmaker, educator and media strategist. However, I must also admit that truth is inherently relative within any story. Isn't a good story merely the sequential reorganization of information (in other words, "editing") so as to make it compelling and efficient to the recipient? At worst, it is a lie – a fiction – because unless it's a sporting competition, uncut, raw reality just isn't interesting enough to attract someone's attention (ask anyone who has participated in a "reality" TV show how facial expressions and words are chopped up and placed out-of-order

to manufacture drama). Technology giant Apple named a
special editing transition in its software "The Ken Burns Effect"
in recognition of the filmmaker's ability to create a magical,
dynamic aura around a static visual. So it's not too surprising
to hear Burns say in *On Story*, "All story is manipulation. Is
there acceptable manipulation? You bet. Truth is, we hope a
byproduct of the best of our stories."

If we've historically used story as a memorable way to
convey information through a narrative structure, we should
also admit that in this quest for emotive impact, the editing
process necessitates the excision of extraneous information that
does not always directly support the underlying premise to the
story. After all, wouldn't the complete, truthful informational
picture be mere data, a series of facts (events, consequences)
lacking momentum, direction or catharsis? In 4 BCE, the Greek
philosopher Aristotle looked for some sort of conflict,
complication, tension or transformation in *Poetics* through his
metaphorical tying of the narrative knot, testimony to the
demands of an interesting story. Without that tension, is there
even a story? Even as we say that a "conflict of interest" is
repugnant in our own interpersonal relationships, we could also
say that there seems to be *little interest without conflict* when it
comes to the stories that help shape those relationships. This

may be why there is little marketability in "good news" devoid of any element of negativity – something I came to understand all too well as a television journalist. Certainly, positive outcomes can be newsworthy when it involves some sort of triumph over adversity. But when was the last time you saw a story on the evening news about the number of planes that landed safely at your local airport? Never. Because that's not a story, it's merely data, something best relegated to airline websites and in-airport informational displays.

"Don't let the facts get in the way of a good story," an old TV journalist hand once told me, only half in jest. I also remember one salty executive producer lamenting the existence of three warring ethnic groups in Bosnia in the mid-1990's: the Serbs, Croats and Muslims. "That's ethnic one group too many," he would say, wondering how we could keep American viewers tuned in to a two-minute story about people living somewhere that few of them could place on a map.

I wish we could assign these inherent shortcomings in storytelling to the 20th century mass media age, with its luxuriously limited number of institutional players feeding content to an attentive, passive audience with too much time on its hands. No one could easily call out this powerful, self-policing bunch of broadcasters and publishers if they played around with the truth, especially if it were in the realm of advertising or entertainment. But our desperation to connect and persuade in the digital age has actually exacerbated our need to accentuate the dramatic, sometimes at the expense of the facts, ethics and good taste. So while good storytelling may be a timeless art, networked technology has introduced a series of new realities.

One way that cable television producers and savvy bloggers have tried to meet these new challenges is through the use of dramatic, definitive lists. They frame the content into digestible chunks through an efficient urgency of "what you need to know." I've played the game myself, publishing "Five Ways to Boost Your Digital Career in 2012" on Mashable.com, a prominent blog about social media, in an effort to promote my graduate program (all five ways implicitly point to submitting an application). So why not create a list of seven "hard truths" about storytelling in a networked world? Why seven? It was a number that emerged only after I had developed the narrative that follows.

Hard Truth #1: We're drowning in data. Stories help make sense of it all.

After all, we've never been awash in more information than we are now. And it's only going to get worse. In "The Case Against Digital Sprawl," (*Bloomberg* "Management Blog," May 2, 2012), IBM's VP of Supercomputing, David Turek shared some astounding statistics about our information affliction. Turek observes, "From the beginning of recorded time until 2003, humans created 5 billion gigabytes of information (five exabytes)." In 2011, we were producing that much every two weeks. Soon he estimates, we will do so every 10 minutes!

This reaction to Turek's post sums up why the information glut only continues to grow, thanks to our proliferation of digital devices:

[E]very time your cell phone sends out its GPS location, every time you buy something online, every time you click the Like button on Facebook, you're putting another digital message in a bottle. And now the oceans are pretty much covered with them.

And that's only part of the story. Text messages, customer records, ATM transactions, security camera images…the list goes on and on. The buzzword to describe this is "Big Data," though that hardly does justice to the scale of the monster we've created (Randy Rieland, "Big Data or Too Much Information?" *Smithsonian.com: Innovations* May 7, 2012)

A responsible storyteller needs to help make sense of all the "Big Data" that we're generating every nanosecond of the day. Indeed, I see a natural connection between the two: the data is a product of our lives as it's now being captured (and produced) by our devices in real-time; stories interpret what we're doing and what it means. Conversely, stories can inspire us to engage and shift our behavior (volunteer, elevate our heart rate during exercise, buy a product, vote a certain way, eat more healthfully) – a shift that is captured and measured through the data.

We can also see all those points of contact and informational exhaust as...noise. To rise above the din with your story, you may be compelled to do something odious: shout louder so that it not only sticks in someone's brain, but they're also shocked into a quick reaction. We might think this is exactly what has been happening for years on websites with online comments; to the point that we've become inured to this form of once-audacious discourse.

Although the stakes keep rising when it comes to what will "go viral," many still see value in the elusive search for the Holy Grail of mass attention. But attaining that level of exposure also make us vulnerable to the highly skeptical, sometimes cynical pushback of web audiences who are only too happy to take a high flier down. In other words, if our content attracts widespread attention, it's also more likely to attract widespread criticism, deconstruction, mimicry and mockery. As storytellers, we can certainly try to inoculate ourselves from this almost intolerable level of withering public glare by focusing on the communication value equation with authenticity (and maybe humor). Thanks to time shifting technology such as digital video recorders and a multitude of streaming media platforms, consumers/users are no longer force-fed content at specific times in specific places. They "opt-in" to the media they choose to consume, especially when it comes to advertising. So now, they'll first ask, "is it worth my time to pay attention to this content, to comment on, be inspired by, to act upon, or share it?"

For they are otherwise a fickle bunch, faced with an abundance of stories, so readily available thanks to YouTube, Netflix, and all those other embeddable players. But how much of our truthfulness as storyteller, or even our mere good intentions are they willing to discount in their quest for a good story? In their need for utility and relevance in the *quid pro quo* exchange for their attention, they seem to be only too happy to suspend disbelief when it comes to the pursuit of distraction through entertainment. Ken Burns offers perhaps a less cynical motivation, "There are many, many different kinds of truths. And an emotional truth is something that you have to build."

Hard Truth #2: Stories necessarily manipulate by bringing order to chaos. The best ones are epic, actionable, personable, tense and empathetic.

The non-profit organization Invisible Children presented online viewers with this sort of value proposition in March 2012, when it uploaded its *Kony 2012* video for public consumption. Within five days, this 30-minute film toppled *Britain's Got Talent* victor Susan Boyle and Old Spice's *The Man Your Man Could Smell Like* advertising campaign as the fastest viral video ever, with 80 million views on YouTube and Vimeo. And then, it imploded, bringing down its creator, along with Invisible Children's ballooning reputation.

Just as the Roman Empire's rise and fall gave history so many teachable moments, *Kony 2012's* much more compressed fate offers those who seek to lead through communication, an opportunity to learn, as we consider what it takes to develop a sustainable storytelling strategy.

As my students know, I'm a big fan of Michael Tierno, whose *Aristotle's Poetics for Screenwriters* (Hyperion, 2002), adapted some of the great thinker's narrative concepts into the *Action-Idea* – in essence, the mission statement of a story. Tierno writes that this story summary of a paragraph or two should be sufficient to "move listeners who merely hear it," powerful enough "so that when it's expanded into a film, a screenplay, whatever, it will hold and move an audience." Ideally, it should have a beginning (premise, status quo), middle (disruption, tension or transformation) and end (resolution, producing a result that differs from the status quo).

I offer this Action-Idea for *Kony 2012*:

An organization devotes its existence to ending the atrocities against children, committed by guerilla warlord Joseph Kony and his Lord's Resistance Army (LRA). It decides that the best way to stop Kony is to make him so famous that governments will be forced to step up their efforts to find him and bring him to justice. Invisible Children produces a 30-minute web video and publishes it, using social media channels to raise awareness, targeting celebrities and policy makers. In this way, they hope to "Cover The Night" in a month through a worldwide urban poster campaign, changing "the conversation of a culture."

As video was introduced to the Web, concern over bandwidth (both technological and human) inspired the generally-accepted commandment "thou shall keep thy video brief, five minutes or less."

But the advent of video portals such as Netflix, Hulu, YouTube and Vimeo, combined with increasingly liberal upload policies (and faster broadband connections) has shattered this directive. Viewers are open to longer-form storytelling, and have become more tolerant of consuming it via online channels, well beyond television. The popularity of tablets such as the iPad, combined with the ever-rising screen resolutions of smartphones, has whetted their appetite for content consumption anytime, anywhere.

Still, this digital media has to correspond to their interests and the pacing has got to be dynamic enough to sustain attention. If as viewers, they're willing to "lean back" and watch that long-form web video on our always connected smart TV, phone or tablet, they're also expecting an experience similar to one they would have in a movie theater or during prime time television viewing.

That's exactly what Invisible Children delivered with *Kony 2012.* I urge anyone who seeks to engage through multimedia storytelling to watch this video, even as I highlight the key narrative points here.

[http://www.youtube.com/watch?v=Y4MnpzG5Sqc]

a. Goes epic, dangles a payoff

The film's director, Jason Russell, also narrates it. He hooks the Internet Generation from the opening frames, with an epic idea, designed to appeal to its desire to be part of something historic: universal connectivity: "There are more people on Facebook than there were on the planet 200 years ago." As most people probably first learned about this film from one of their friends through a social media platform, this was a clever opening gambit.

Russell then smartly sets expectations as to how much attention should be budgeted for his creation. He inserts a clock and informs viewers that this film will last another 27 minutes. And then he brings them in as insiders, that by watching this, they become willing participants in a grand "experiment" that will only work if they pay attention. He both laid down a challenge, and created enough intrigue to incite people to delve a little deeper.

b. Gets personal

The film's director continues to tug at collective heartstrings by sharing a video clip from the birth of his son Gavin. "Every single person in the world started this way…because he's here, he matters." Obviously, you can't go wrong with images of cute kids. But Russell is also using the relationship with his son (and their on-camera conversation) to prepare viewers to start caring about the plight of a Ugandan boy, half a world away. It's an intimate connection that's easy to make, compared to the habitual "here's an unfortunate African child that you should care about."

c. Sets the conflict

Russell takes a few minutes to set the stage to his story, but then quickly escalates the tension by introducing Jacob, a young survivor of the atrocities of the Lord's Resistance Army (LRA) in Uganda. Fortunately, he has video from his initial encounter with Jacob, ten years earlier; the night Jacob escaped the village after his brother was murdered by the LRA. Jacob tells Russell that he wish he would have died, as his brother did. "We may meet in heaven," he says, and starts to cry. The soundtrack's soft strings swell. Russell tells Jacob, "We are going to do everything that we can to stop them. Do you hear my words?"

d. Brings viewers along for the journey

By now, he has hooked his viewers. Their hearts should be in their mouths; they may even feel guilty that they've never heard about the child soldier affliction in East Africa until now. "If this had gone on in America, it'd be on the cover of Newsweek" Russell says to Jacob at one point.

That's when the filmmaker turns the tables. He says this movie is no longer about him, or even Jacob; that it's now about those who are watching. He even clarifies their limited time to act, adding that the movie "expires" on December 31st. Online "deal" sites also use this artificial restriction – it's a way of galvanizing attention and accelerating a need to take action. The payoff should they decide to collaborate with Invisible Children is a "chance to change human history" no less. All they have to do is stop Joseph Kony (the film's latter half builds the case against the Ugandan warlord). And the narrator is going to explain exactly how to do it.

Invisible Children believes that steady and unrelenting pressure on world governments (especially America's) will step up the search for Kony. But that's too elusive an objective for a revved up public in an on-demand world, which has been inspired to do something. So the film offers three simple actionable items: sign the online pledge, get the "Action Kit" via a donation through the Invisible Children website, and/or share the movie. On top of that, the organization leveraged social media channels urging those who had watched the film to contact twelve key global policy makers, or re-transmit pre-written Tweets to a series of influential celebrities.

Russell ends the storyline by returning to the simple intimacy of conversation with his son. He says that he wants to make the world a better place for Gavin. It's a simple goal, one that many parents harbor for their own children. "I'm going to be like you Dad," Gavin says as the film concludes. "When you grow up?" Russell asks. "Yeah" the boy replies. "Are you sure?" he asks, as it turns out, not unreasonably.

Hard Truth #3: Storytellers may avail themselves of an audience's goodwill – but only for a limited time.

Kony 2012's 100-plus million views is testimony to how much the story resonated deeply among (primarily younger) people. But that exceptional popularity also brought harsh scrutiny. Seasoned Uganda experts began to weigh in: the film was an oversimplification of a complex situation; it was placing undue emphasis on a conflict that had subsided (Kony had been driven from Uganda five years earlier); rather than emphasize the hunt for Kony, why not put funds towards the rehabilitation of his young victims? And there were also accusations of colonialism from Ugandans who had watched the film and wondered why their country was being so unfairly represented.

The film's overnight success propelled Russell into international stardom, also increasingly subjecting him to critical questions under harsh television network lights – which would be a highly stressful situation for almost anyone. A few days later, he was arrested after what appeared to be a nervous breakdown. He was found naked, ranting publicly on a street corner. By then, the popularity of *Kony 2012* had already plummeted after the initial surge of interest. Invisible Children released a follow-up film, one month later, with a different narrator responding to some of the public criticism from the first. It garnered fewer than two million views -- still an impressive number, but a tiny fraction of the original video's success.

By all accounts, the April 20ᵗʰ "Cover the Night" campaign that the films had sought to incite was a bust. In Seattle, I spotted only two *Kony 2012* posters, hidden away under a bridge adjacent to my university campus. At the same time, the group's Facebook page filled up with critical, sometimes insulting, comments. The world had moved on just as quickly as it had fallen for Invisible Children. *The Guardian*, a British newspaper, compiled an excellent "Reality Check: Kony 2012" series of articles and analyses if you'd like to find out more about the film's impact.

[http://www.guardian.co.uk/news/series/reality-check-kony-2012]

In this world of effortless communication, it truly is "easy come, easy go." *The New York Times'* media reporter, Brian Stelter, called out this new news cycle in "From Flash to Fizzle" (April 14, 2012), with "individual bursts of light that appear out of nowhere and disappear just as fast." Stelter attributed this phenomenon to the continuing commoditization of news – a bulk product whose origin brings little additional value – and how it is shared through social networks. The "new" needs to stand out more than ever to retain its visibility within the data deluge; audiences are so easily distracted by the next big thing that comes along. "Of the 7.1 million page views of Wikipedia's article on Mr. Kony so far this year, 5 million were racked up in the three days when the video was a hot topic online. Now it's viewed fewer than 15,000 times a day," Stelter observed.

This may explain the so-called "slacktivism" of our age, with frictionless interactivity that makes it so easy to learn more about something that elicits concern, facilitates the ability to share relevant content or just express an outrage, and just as quickly move on because the communication transaction required so little up front investment. This action/reaction cycle is only going to get faster thanks to the ever increasing utility of mobile devices. An April 2012 *Pew Internet Project* report ("Digital Differences") observed:

Once someone has a wireless device, she becomes much more active in how she uses the Internet–not just with wireless connectivity, but also with wired devices. The same holds true for the impact of wireless connections and people's interest in using the Internet to connect with others. These mobile users go online not just to find information but to share what they find and even create new content much more than they did before.

So what's the takeaway for storytellers? If you've managed to inspire the public to take action after you've recounted your story, you also need to make it as simple as possible for them to act and react. The American Red Cross did exactly this after hours after the devastating January 2010 earthquake in Haiti. It set up a "Text Haiti to 90999" program, widely publicized on broadcast networks and social media platforms, and coordinated through a partnership with the National Football League. It raised $32 million through this channel, 7% of the total overall funds it received (see Dan Butcher, "American Red Cross adjusts mobile giving strategy post-Haiti," *Mobile Commerce Daily*, February 17, 2011).

Now that 46% of American adults own smartphones, it's young adults who have the highest level of smartphone ownership, "regardless of income or educational attainment." This is precisely the demographic group that responded most strongly to *Kony 2012* and it speaks to how they will increasingly connect, share and create with each other through these powerful, ubiquitously connected devices.

Hard Truth #4: Attention-grabbing lies that devalue the audience payoff will push them away. Be genuine.

So if this is the new reality of our "attention economy" we have to make the best of a temporary jackpot should we be so skillful or lucky "go viral" with our content. We also need to be prepared for a possible backlash. This accentuates the need to get our facts straight at the outset, or at the very least, avoid raising suspicions that we weren't about to "let the facts get in the way of a good story." It's telling that Invisible Children's more accurate, detail-filled follow-up to *Kony 2012* failed to resonate at the same level as its predecessor. It begs the question whether *Kony 2012* would have gone viral had it actually accounted for the criticism it would later receive and modified its script. What if it had clearly outlined that Kony was no longer in Uganda, that there were other organizations on the ground that were working with victims of the LRA, and that there were relatively few soldiers left in Kony's army? Without the imminent threat of its bogeyman, tied to the reality that Invisible Children wasn't a lonely group of determined activists, it's hard to believe that this story would have been as impactful as it was. Certainly, Invisible Children raised a great deal of awareness through its campaign (and money), but was the price too high, with a massive hit to its reputation?

This highlights an inherent shortcoming of story as a vehicle to engage others: that the public will wonder whether we're being genuine, especially if there's a big ask and emotions are in play. They may accept the lie, but only for so long. If that lie devalues the payoff, then they may just as quickly move on. And yet, we still need to edit, polish and maintain a sharp focus if we're going to remain true to our Action-Idea. This may be the unpalatable truth underlying our reliance on story as a conveyor of information. However, as master fiction storyteller Neil Gaiman points out in his now-classic *American Gods* (William Morrow, 2001) novel, the entertainment-information bargain is one that humanity has made for centuries, eyes wide open:

We need individual stories. Without individuals, we see only numbers. A thousand dead. A hundred thousand dead. "Casualties may rise to a million." With individual stories, the statistics become people. But even that is a lie. For the people continue to suffer in numbers that themselves are numbing and meaningless. Look. See the child's swollen belly and the flies that crawl at the corners of his eyes -- his skeletal limbs. Will it make it easier for you to know his name? His age? His dreams? His fears? To see him from the inside?

And if it does are we not doing a disservice to his sister who lies in the searing dust beside him, a distorted, distended caricature of a human child? And there, if we feel for them, are they not more important to us than a thousand other children touched by the same famine, a thousand other young lives who will soon be food for the flies own myriad squirming children.

...Fiction allows us to slide into these other heads, these other places, and look out through other eyes. And in the tale, we stop before we die, or we die vicariously and unharmed. And in the world beyond the tale, we turn the page or close the book and we resume our lives.

Perhaps this is what Ken Burns means when he speaks of "emotional truth" being an acceptable form of the truth, as we continually try "to keep the wolf from the door."

Berkman Center for Internet and Society researcher Ethan Zuckerman struggled with this entertainment-information conundrum himself, in his superb blog *My Heart's in Accra* ("The Passion of Mike Daisey: Journalism, Storytelling and the Ethics of Attention," March 28, 2012)

He criticized Invisible Children's oversimplification, even as he connected it to the commensurate discovery that monologist Mike Daisey had made up several key facts about Apple's seemingly inhumane labor practices in its Chinese factories. Daisey's nationally popular one-man performance *The Agony and the Ecstasy of Steve Jobs*, was perceived by many a serious journalist as a truthful documentary, leading most famously to a National Public Radio (NPR) feature on *This American Life*. The show was later forced to apologize and retract the story after another NPR journalist outed Daisey in his investigation.

Zuckerman had to grapple with the fundamental question: did the ends justify the means? If this new world, soaked with content presents unique challenges to attract attention, is there not virtue in having discovered a way for the public to care about a particular issue? And what if they cared so much that they were actually moved to actually take action in response?

"I think it's possible to admire that Invisible Children used social media brilliantly and made an evocative and affecting film while being angry that the film was manipulative and upset about the lack of Ugandan voices. Invisible Children were doing their job in advocating for their cause," Zuckerman wrote.

Clearly, Invisible Children was practicing advocacy and not journalism. But as journalism has morphed into just another form of content to be consumed and shared online, it's increasingly difficult to distinguish between fact and fiction when a media-savvy organization such as Invisible Children produces such an engaging pseudo-documentary. Zuckerman concludes that these controversies mark a shift in the conversation about attention. "The conversation has involved web publishers, advertisers and activists all asking how we compete successfully for small slices of attention. With stories like Daisey's and *Kony 2012*, the conversation switches from the practical question of seizing attention to the ethical questions of attention."

Hard Truth #5: A good story is just the beginning. You've got to network that narrative.

As the Internet became a more mainstream medium, a few seasoned users expressed optimism that these new technologies, tied to a universally set of networks, would activate billions of new voices, enabled by this ubiquitously available communication machinery (in particular the authors of the 1999 *Cluetrain Manifesto*, and Yochai Benkler in his excellent 2006 book, *The Wealth of Networks*). In many ways this has occurred. Yet, the challenge now is with so many people chatting, creating, transmitting, there seem to be fewer who are actually listening. There's no guarantee of "build it and they will come" – that a great piece of content will necessarily find an audience. Perhaps this is why that last successful holdout of legacy media – television – continues to thrive. Despite fragmentation due to cable and satellite, television is still a place that aggregates attention and eyeballs – even if particular niche channels only attract tens of thousands of viewers at a given time. This last great mass media water cooler, tied to new "second screen" technology (notably tablets) facilitates the consumption and sharing of content. This new functionality has stayed television's reckoning for the time being. It doesn't hurt that viewers (especially in the United States, where TV consumption continues to rise) continue to want to "lean back" after a hard day and passively consume content. The Nielsen *Television Audience Report for 2010 & 2011* observes that household viewership actually has increased, to a staggering 59 hours and 28 minutes per week in 2011, but television ownership has actually decreased (not by much, but still, that's remarkable given that the growing U.S. population). Meanwhile, another Pew Research study ("The Rise of the 'Connected Viewer,'" July 17, 2012) reveals that 52% of Americans use their cellphone while watching television, visiting websites mentioned on television, seeing what other people were saying online about a program, or even posting comments online about the program. Yet again, young people (18-24) are singled out for dramatic use of these new technologies, with 81% of this demographic using cellphones while watching television.

The proliferation of use of these portable networking devices means that smartphone users in particular are now extending their Internet connectivity well beyond their traditional places of connection: the home and the office. They're no longer shackled by their relatively cumbersome personal computers and their broadband connections, which means they're less likely to "hang up" on the world. This is especially true as social media platforms increase the incentive to want to remain connected, even as the smartphone with its apps and so-called unlimited data plans facilitate the ability to whet that desire. The consequences of this were readily on display at the 2012 Consumer Electronics Show (CES). Over 150,000 people and 3,100 exhibitors descended upon Las Vegas (a record number), many of them recognizing that the game has changed thanks to these relatively inexpensive but powerful devices that so much of the developed world now has in its pockets and purses. They see that consumers want access to data and content at our convenience, and that they value the enhanced utility that these new technologies bring. Not only are they moving away from home and office as their terrestrial digital headquarters, they're also moving away from technologies that favored the enterprise (the stability, security and predictability of say a Windows computer or a Blackberry smartphone) to a more consumer-driven world that emphasizes sociability, creativity and entertainment (such as the iPhone, YouTube and Facebook).

This convergence of device and platform is not just about entertainment and the connected screen. Rather, there are countless applications in safety and security, energy management, health and wellbeing. I saw this firsthand at CES when I checked out in-vehicle technology demonstrations at Ford and Mercedes. We will soon be able to integrate the functionality, connectivity, CPU power and portability of our smartphones into our cars, kitchens and fitness routines. Imagine driving down a city street as a virtual display on your windshield notifies you that one of your social media "friends" is ahead of you, three cars down. Would you like to invite her for lunch at a nearby, highly rated restaurant (according to Yelp)? Did you also notice that your car's entertainment system just tuned into the song streaming at the bar you just drove by. Go ahead; add it to your "favorites" with a swipe through the air. Hopefully, it's not too heart-pounding a tune, as your car's wellness systems are monitoring your stress levels, pulse and reaction time. By the way, you're headed to the supermarket, where you'll have a grocery list, waiting on your smartphone, auto-generated by the real-time inventory system on your smart fridge at home. Should you be worried that the kids have forgotten where to find that snack you left for them, don't hesitate to scrawl a quick note on your phone's screen, which will materialize instantaneously on the fridge's in-door monitor – the kitchen's cork board of the 21st century. You remark to yourself that as all this technology becomes more pervasive, you seem to notice it less as well. It just does what you expect it to, fitting neatly into the routine of your life, as all appliances do. Ultimately, this wholesale transformation of our world, incited primarily by these technologies, leads to fewer "how do I?" questions, and increasingly to more strategic, or philosophical "what does this mean?"

Navigating this new world requires a keen understanding of the forces at play: how social networks function, identifying influencers, learning how to collaborate in new ways, extracting stories from all the data that this 24/7 online behavior is generating, monitored and captured in real time, all the time, into the cloud.

In this ecosystem, success is derived from the smart management of the rules of engagement even as Ethan Zuckerman's "small slices of attention" perpetually challenge us to maintain that engagement and convert it into something actionable.

Kony 2012's massive initial success in capturing so much of that diminishing reserve of attention gives us a glimpse of what is to come. Award-winning television producer and media consultant Drew Keller focuses specifically on channel creation around content. Keller, who also teaches storytelling for the graduate program that I direct, was especially taken with the social media analysis conducted by measurement agency Social

Flow, which created a network graph of the Twitter updates at the height of the campaign's popularity. Interestingly, the wave began in the so-called American "heartland," and not in the traditional media capitals of New York, Los Angeles, Miami, Chicago, etc. It was in Oklahoma City, Pittsburgh and Noblesville, Indiana where a Christian organization such as Invisible Children could nurture its strongest networks, relying on its deep ties to youth groups and churches. This is "bonding" social capital, leveraging pre-existing, like-minded social networks, inspiring them to talk about and share the *Kony 2012* film among themselves. But to go viral where social network researcher Dana Boyd observes "attention begets attention," a storyteller needs to create strong "bridging" social capital reaching out to other communities that would not normally fall into your sphere of influence, because of divergent interests or lack of social proximity. Here's Keller's perspective on how Invisible Children brilliantly deployed its content and networks to spread the word around *Kony 2012*.

"Contrary to initial media reports, *Kony 2012* didn't randomly drop out of the sky into this community. Invisible Children was connecting and communicating actively with these participants for at least a year prior to the video's release.

Its team also created interest and "buzz" around the video in the days prior to posting the video, not unlike a movie studio creates buzz for an upcoming feature. There were social media postings telling the audience to "get ready" for something important. By nurturing the community, and giving them inside information, they engaged their preexisting community to feel they had inside information, that they were part of something special, that they were unique and chosen. Invisible Children effectively primed the pump with a sympathetic audience predisposed to share. They, in essence, created an effective syndication model where they only needed to release the video to a well-defined target audience and their community would do the work. The second strategy that is important to remember is they made it very easy to share a syndication message across multiple networks. For example, they created a link matrix on the Invisible Children website with photos of pop icons where a community member needed only to click on a URL to send out a preformatted tweet to a celebrity. This effectively buried the celebrities with Twitter messages, causing many to engage in the communication stream with positive messages about the video, buying credibility in *Kony 2012* from the pop icon.

It also gamed the Twitter system for trending topics, creating an artificial number of tweets around the #KONY2012 hashtag. People who were not a target of the celebrity tweets, nor were part of the initial Invisible Children social media community, took notice of the traffic and began to watch the video. As they engaged in the social media stream the trending topic began to take on its own specific gravity."

Hard Truth #6: Own your story before the platform owns you (if you value independence and the relationships that you inspire).

As Keller observes, despite all the challenges that would follow, Invisible Children had succeeded in creating a story that would connect, inspire and encourage its supporters to "spread the gospel" of *Kony 2012*. Obviously, I've embraced the benefits of how a handful of these social media platforms (Facebook and Twitter are the usual suspects, but there are highly successful non-American social utilities, such as China's Sina Weibo) have greatly facilitated this form of content sharing. But even as the "conversation" in all this "conversational marketing" gains currency as digital platforms and devices become more pervasive, the danger is that we professionals rely too much on network-building strategies that depend on those few digital platforms. These channels inspire more chatter than content production — quickly satiating a population's creative urges without truly compelling them to be creative, let alone verbose with space restrictions on status updates, such as Twitter's 140 characters.

On top of that, I object to how companies such as Facebook lay claim to the content that we do share, with overly complicated terms of service and a propensity to encourage us to give it all away. Now that Facebook has gone public with its multi-billion dollar valuation, we now see how much value this sharing brings to it. It's no wonder that *The New York Times* says that "personal data is the oil of the digital age" (Joshua Brustein, "Start-Ups Seek to Help Users Put a Price on Their Personal Data," February 12, 2012).

I don't hate Facebook. I just don't trust it. I refuse to use it as a "social utility" to track my actions throughout the web. I won't tell it my real birthday, my true "likes" or my favorite music. When the "Timeline" feature went live, I realized that Facebook was increasingly tricking me into making my posts public. So I canceled my five year-old account once Facebook announced that it would seek an Initial Public Offering. I wanted to wipe out all that data that overly exposed my family (my two children were born during that period) and friends.

If Facebook wants to make money off of me, I believe that as a professional who earns a living from the content that I produce, it's only fair that I should reciprocate. So similar to how I use Twitter and Google +, I created a new account, primarily for professional relationships. I allow anyone to subscribe to me, and I'm liberal in who I friend (which I had been careful about previously), because I have less to worry about. Now, it doesn't matter whether I trust Facebook or not.

I no longer post images directly to my account. It doesn't get a royalty-free license over my photo, it can't make money off of it, and it will not subject it to facial recognition algorithms. Rather, I upload them directly to my WordPress blog, where my ownership rights are clear.

At the same time, I pledged to put more time and thought into creating what I do want to share. I do not limit myself to 140 characters. I do not concern myself with how I present myself in the relative blandness of online suburbia (cartoonist Hugh MacLeod declared "Facebook is the new suburbia" in his gapingvoid.com blog on December 29, 2011). I hope to tell more stories, and to share more insights.

All of this had inspired me to come up with my own Terms of Service for *my* personal data:

1. The content that I create is mine.

2. You may benefit from my data, but only the data that I expressly share with you as part of an equally weighted value proposition. I get to use your service to fulfill a certain personal or professional objective; you get my data.

3. I will only share things online that I would normally publicly express in a conversation, a lecture, or in writing — unless I truly just want to give away for public benefit (ideally under a Creative Commons license).

4. Ideally, you should pay me for the use of "online me" in all other cases.

I believe that this entrepreneurial independence and emphasis on ownership is fundamental to our ability to remain nimble and innovative in a time when systems remain in flux. This is a transformative period, with business models being turned upside down – from publishing to politics, entertainment to higher education. Digital networks have facilitated a whole new kind of collaboration that can lead to powerful outcomes: the Arab Spring uprising in the Middle East is a recent example of this, where Facebook, YouTube, Twitter and the blogosphere accelerated political change in sclerotic regimes (Tunisia, Egypt) through collaboration and facilitated communication among activists. Yet, at the same time, the gold rush is now as big money tries to lay claim to those very same networks. And some of those platforms may not necessarily guarantee privacy or unfettered use when larger business questions come into play. Beyond that, they may not be able to control how less-than-democratic governments gain access to their citizens' data.

The so-called "YouTube" war in Syria in 2012 is evidence as to how complex this has become. Less than a decade earlier, I was reporting from Damascus for NBC News, just after Baghdad had fallen to the U.S. military. Syria was concerned that it could just as easily succumb to such an invasion; the Syrian government expected me to file my reports from its government-controlled TV station as a way to keep tabs on me. But more often than not, I availed myself of a satellite phone uplink hidden behind my hotel room curtains to upload video reports to New York.

Syrian rebels have been using similar methods to get their side of the story out, but this time uploading their films to YouTube. These amateur soldiers also turned to the social web to learn how to use their weapons (Spencer Ackerman, "Syrian Rebels Use YouTube, Facebook for Weapons Training, *Wired.com Danger Room*, July 17, 2012). *The New York Times* has curated YouTube footage on its "Watching Syria's War" page because foreign journalists have been mostly banned from entering Syria (a famous exception was the undercover documentary *Syria: Songs of Defiance* than an undercover Al-Jazeera journalist shot on his iPhone). J. David Goodman links to videos from citizen journalists who are against the Syrian regime, as well as official government stories, only after analyzing them and trying to get an initial read on their credibility. "For me, the most important issue is to present each video without claiming it is fact," Goodman told *TechPresident* (Lisa Goldman, "How the New York Times Uses Citizen Media to Watch Syria's War," July 16, 2012). "Even when we believe the video is accurate, we want our readers to know that we didn't shoot it so we can't take responsibility for it. And of course these videos are presented by people [in Syria] who have a point of view - an agenda. So we present context and explain why we cannot say 100 percent that it's true."

Still, though the Arab Spring in neighboring countries may have inspired the uprising in Syria, social media sites are treacherous. The Syrian government stopped blocking Facebook, YouTube and Twitter in 2011, only to unleash sophisticated surveillance equipment to monitor users, particularly from those visiting sites sympathetic to the rebellion:

Luring opposition sympathizers with tainted video links in e-mail, fake Skype encryption tools, tainted online documents, hackers believed to be allied to Syria's government have in recent months deployed an array of powerful spyware with names like DarkComet, backdoor.bruet, and Blackshades. Available on the Internet, these malware are used to infiltrate the personal computers of opposition figures and rights activists and send back information on their friends and contacts as well as passwords, cybersecurity experts say. The impact of this spying is hard to gauge. But even as the physical battle intensifies in and around Damascus, Syria cyber watchers are worried (Mark Clayton, "Syria's cyberwars: using social media against dissent," *The Christian Science Monitor*, July 25, 2012).

As I've argued here (and elsewhere), both the challenge and opportunity in today's communication ecosystem is how to build creative persuasive, trustful relationships. Connecting to people, communities and networks in relevant, useful ways is how we sell products and services, win votes, encourage healthful behavior, inspire civic virtue. That's the heart of communication in the 21st century for professionals, and how we manage those relationships is how we lead in this transformational, tumultuous era. Retaining control over our content and data – and maintaining strategic perspective on how to employ it – is crucial to our success as leaders in any organization. Though we understand the benefits that many of these social platforms bring to our communication needs, we must ultimately keep our eyes wide open as to their full ramifications.

Hard Truth #7: Inspirational storytelling can lead to powerful collaboration, and still leave you in command.

My antidote to the disequilibrium of *Kony 2012's* odd success is a much smaller story that inspired a heartwarming call to action, as well as a rich Return on Investment (ROI). The storyteller's immediate challenge was how to attract attention to a remarkable nine year-old boy's arcade of homemade games, fashioned from repurposed cardboard boxes. The storyteller-as-leader's larger objective was to raise $25,000 for the boy's college fund.

Nirvan Mullick was a struggling filmmaker who was searching for a door handle for his old Toyota, when he discovered Caine Monroy's cardboard arcade behind his father's auto parts shop in East Los Angeles. He was taken with the boy's entrepreneurial spirit, who was selling passes to play the makeshift games he had crafted from the shop's discarded boxes ($1 for four turns, or $2 for a 500-turn "Fun Pass"). Mullick was surprised to learn that he was the first to buy a ticket. This was due to a dearth of foot traffic in the area, and because Caine's father made most of his sales online.

Mullick was inspired to change that situation. He orchestrated a surprise flash mob to descend upon the arcade and surprise Caine. He first posted the happening as an event on the Facebook page "Hidden Los Angeles" with over 200,000 followers. It went viral within the first hour, then quickly showed up on Reddit.com (the self-proclaimed "front page of the Internet"). He captured it all on camera.

Mullick posted the film to YouTube and Vimeo on April 9th 2012, just as the *Kony 2012* sensation was fading into oblivion. By the first night, Mullick's work had raised $6,000 for Caine's scholarship fund. As I write this, he has raised over $200,000, almost ten times his original goal, which now goes to a foundation to "fund creativity and entrepreneurship in kids."

The film's Action-Idea is simple:

A young boy decides to build an arcade with the discarded boxes from his father's struggling auto parts store. A filmmaker visits the store, and discovers the boy's arcade. He's surprised to learn that he's the boy's first paying customer, and decides to do something about it, inspired by the boy's ingenuity and can-do spirit. A flash mob descends upon the arcade, and plays all day, to the delight of its owner.

While Mullick has availed himself of Facebook and Twitter to spread the word, cainesarcade.com resides on the open source blogging platform WordPress (which I also use for my *Storyteller Uprising* site). I'm gratified that the filmmaker has embedded the film through Vimeo, which gets a fraction of the views that YouTube does, but is a place where the film community likes to upload its work. The film has received 3.5 million views on Vimeo, and 3 million on YouTube.

[http://vimeo.com/40000072]

It's a strategy that led to a simple call to action: donate to change this young person's life, and an amazing ROI through a simple, yet powerful story.

This idea of resolving a larger business-related challenge through a story strategy is exactly what the U.S. Army has done over the last few years with its successful Army Strong Stories program. As social media became more popular, the Army realized that online conversations were occurring and it had no formal mechanism to respond (let alone control those conversations). It was concerned that some of what was being said was inaccurate, which might have a negative effect on its recruiting efforts as well as on the general sentiment towards the organization.

So in collaboration with its public relations agency, Weber Shandwick (I have worked with the agency in the past, which is how I learned about this client), it decided to tell its own stories. The Army hoped that it would humanize its mission, as well as build trust and foster conversation among prospective recruits, and media influencers. It would do so through the unvarnished stories of nearly 900 of its own soldiers through a blogging platform and short videos. Soldiers also interact with each other, all through www.armystrongstories.com. The stories are syndicated through social platforms such as Facebook and YouTube, but the website remains the primary repository for the stories and the conversations around them. Here's one comment in response to a blog post that demonstrates how the organization's recruiting objectives are being met through the platform:

Major Grimes,
You likely do not remember me, but 2 years ago we had a
conversation on this blog about the Army JAG application process. I
have applied every year and as a 3L I have applied for an active duty
commission. I understand the competition is tough, but I believe I can
contribute to the Army.
I wanted to thank you for the helpful advice, which I employed in my
application and law school tenure. I hope you're enjoying your new
Army role and congratulations on the new baby.
Regards,
Thomas Grier
3L The Ohio State University Moritz College of Law
(Benjamin Grimes, "A Brief Return to the Recruiting Trenches,"
ArmyStrongStories.com, November 9, 2011)

The site also serves as an internal conversational channel for those who are already inside the U.S. Army's community. Here's an excerpt from a well-written post by a military spouse as her husband is about to leave for another deployment:

"Hey," I say placing my forehead to his.
"Hey," he replies.
"You doing alright?" I ask. Stupid question, I know.
"Yeah." He lies.
I lean back to look into his eyes, the eyes I first noticed the day we met. I drowned that day and with it died my loneliness. I hope he will bear with me while I speak.
"I need you to do something for me." I warn with a smile as if he's not doing enough.
His brows nearly touch as he declares, "anything." Of course anything, he wouldn't do less.
"Listen and let me finish before you speak." I advise with a cautious smile. He nods looking a bit confused.
"I am going to kiss you," I say and he grins. "You're going to look into my eyes and remember everything you see. The love the pride and the confidence I have in you." It takes every cell in my body to hold things together and I can feel a headache coming on from stealing my tears. I continue, "then you're going to close your eyes and picture me and boys and how much fun we had this morning. When you open them again, I'll be gone." (Kimberlee Thomas, "My Sacrifice" ArmyStrongStories.com, April 24, 2012)

Because this organization decided to leverage the power of the real and authentic stories of its own constituents, what started as a site, is now a sophisticated mechanism to syndicate this persuasive content throughout the Army's various media platforms (including broadcast). It's an amazing achievement for a military organization that traditionally had a tendency to suppress unofficial communication that wasn't uttered by someone at top of the chain of command. It's also a tacit recognition that expectations around communication have changed because of networked technologies, and the organizations themselves must also change to stay relevant during these transformational times. Even as we must grapple with this new form of communication, we must do the same with a new type of leadership.

Media strategist Charlene Li calls this "Open Leadership" and uses it as a term as the title for her book. It's an exhortation to leaders to abandon their traditional need to maintain tight control over their organizations and staff.

"They should instead be asking, 'How do I develop the kind of new, open engaged relationships I need to get things done? What's changed today is that new technologies allow us to let go of control and still be in command, because better, cheaper communication tools give us the ability to be intimately familiar with what is happening with both customers and employees" (*Open Leadership*, Jossey-Bass, 2010).

For Li, "open leadership" is about surrendering control in order to *inspire* commitment to accomplish key strategic goals. Whether within an organization or a community, that inspiration should come initially from powerful, successful storytelling -- hard truths and all.

Storyteller Uprising is an ongoing exploration of digital publishing platforms. This published book resides on just one platform. For the latest: http://www.storytelleruprising.com.